Second Edition

THE ABC'S OF WINE, BREW AND SPIRITS

All You Need to Know to Converse and Consume

GENE FORD

Illustrations by Don Wessman

MURRAY PUBLISHERS
Seattle

*Here's to my family...
and that stern virtue—
temperance*

Second Edition

©Copyright 1980 Gene Ford
All rights reserved. No part of this work covered by the copyrights hereon may be reproduced or copied in any form or by any means—graphic, electronic, or mechanical, including photocopying, recording, taping, or information and retrieval systems without written permission of the publisher or author.

ISBN: 0-931754-10-0

Published by
Murray Publishing Company, Inc.
2312 Third Avenue
Seattle, Washington 98121

Contents

A Point of View 5
How it All Happens 7
A Mini Chronology on the Alcohols We Consume 11
    Ancient Times to 500 AD 11
    Medieval Times to 1500 AD 12
    Early Modern Times, 1500 to 1700 AD 13
    Late Modern Times, 1700 to 1980 15
How to Choose the Right Spirit 17
Basic Definitions You Will Need 23
Wine and Liquor—the ABC's 27–116
The Proof of Things 117
Calories and Sugar Levels 118
Beverage Tasting Simplified 119
Five Easy Steps to a Relaxed Wine Tasting Party 121
Cheese and Wine—the Happy Marriage 123
Cordials and Liqueurs by Taste 124
Know Your Limits 125
All That's Needed in Glassware and Equipment 126
    Tools of the Trade 126
    Universal Glassware 127
How to Tend Bar While Smiling and Talking 127
In Case You Wanted to Know More About...
    Brews 129
    Wines 129
    Spirits 129
Or Some Excellent Books 130
Read Those Labels 130
Ford's Garrulous Generalizations On Wine Buying 131
Pronunciations of Common Words 133
Index of Questions by Category 135

A Point of View

*IF ALL BE TRUE THAT I DO THINK,
THERE ARE FIVE REASONS WE SHOULD
DRINK.
GOOD WINE, A FRIEND, OR BEING DRY:
OR LEST WE SHOULD BE BY AND BY:
OR ANY OTHER REASON WHY.*
—Latin Epigram

*OH, GOD, THAT MEN SHOULD PUT AN
ENEMY IN THEIR MOUTHS TO STEAL
AWAY THEIR BRAINS. THAT WE
SHOULD,
WITH JOY, PLEASURE, REVEL AND AP-
PLAUSE, TRANSFORM OURSELVES INTO
BEASTS.*
—William Shakespeare

Perhaps nothing in man's rich history has more profoundly affected his well-being than liquor—for good as well as for evil. As a pleasant release from the anxieties of the day, or as a voracious, consuming addiction, liquor is—and most certainly will be—a constant in the lives of men.

It is sufficient for us to recognize and to accept the enormous impact of beverage alcohol upon our society. Nearly two million of our fellow citizens are employed in making, transporting and selling spirits. Retail sales exceed 32 billions of dollars annually. Federal and local taxes generate over nine and a half billions each year. It is a usurious fact that taxes amount to about three times the manufactured cost of the product!

Yet, America's overall alcoholic consumption has levelled off in recent years. In all forms, we consume each year about 2.7 gallons for every person over 14 years of age. That may seem a lot, but compare it to Portugal's 6.2 gallons; France's 5.9 gallons; or Germany's 3.9 gallons per person. Admittedly, these others are wine imbibing nations! In our pioneer years, we Americans consumed over 7 gallons per person, so we have moderated considerably.

In terms of abuse, there is a considerable body of professional opinion that cultural ignorance may be a causal factor. A director of the National Institute of Alcohol Abuse and Alcoholism has stated that society, rather than individuals may be the greatest cause of alcoholism. He wrote of findings that societies which have alcohol commonly in the diet—those that sip their alcohols slowly and generally with food in relaxed, comfortable surroundings—have a lower incidence of alcoholism.

The urbane commentator Gilbert Chesterton once said that the two things people did not wish to discuss were religion and politics and that these were the only two things worth talking about! Mr. Chesterton should have added alcohol to his list! There is some evidence that we are emerging from the dark ages in the treatment of alcohol consumption. The point of view of this book is that beverage alcohol as a chemical substance is neither good nor evil. Its uses and abuses, however, are profound commentaries on contemporary society.

Temperance and moderation are the companions of knowledge. We will become more moderate in our use of alcohol as we increase our understanding of the workings of the chemical in our system. This book is directed toward that worthy end.

How It All Happens

*QUICKLY, BRING ME A BEAKER OF WINE,
SO THAT I MAY WET MY MIND AND SAY
SOMETHING CLEVER.*
— Aristophanes

*WINE IS CONSTANT PROOF THAT GOD
LOVES US AND LOVES TO SEE US HAPPY.*
— Benjamin Franklin

Above all, one must clearly understand fermentation and distillation. These two chemical functions, one natural and the other artificially contrived, are the fundamental building blocks of liquor sophistication.

First, visualize a tub of freshly harvested wine grapes. They are luscious, juicy sweet to the taste, and each berry is covered with a wax-like bloom. That sticky substance on the skins traps millions of air-born, microscopic, plant-like organisms. These vital cells are commonly known as yeast.

When the grapes are crushed and the skins broken, the yeast cells enter into the grape juice and begin to break down the natural grape sugars. The thousands of yeast cells rapidly become millions. This process of sugar breakdown is called fermentation. In fermentation, enzymes are secreted by the yeast cells which transform the sugars into almost equal parts of ethyl alcohol and carbon dioxide.

Enzyme is a Greek word meaning "in yeast." Enzymes are non-living materials essential to all biological systems. In fermentation, there are at least twelve distinct enzymatic actions. So, grape fermentation is a quite complex chemical process. After fermentation ceases, the alcohol remains in the must with the spent yeast. The carbon dioxide has floated off into the atmosphere.

Fermentation, then, is a natural process. It can and does occur in the absence of man's guiding hand. If a bird pecks open the skin of a grape, the yeast on the skin can enter the grape and make wine in the vineyard.

But, man is now very much involved in this process. To assure a more stable, longer and more productive fermentation period, most American winemakers wash away the wild yeasts from the skins and impregnate the juice with one or more predictable cultured yeasts.

The process is still natural as this special yeast is also one of those found in the field. Since the winemaker harvests his grapes at the precise moment when they achieve the best balance of sugars and acids and he conducts the fermentation in laboratory conditions, his wines are very predictable and quite refined.

The rule of thumb to remember is that the alcohol level in wine is approximately one-half the volume of sugar in the grapes. Wine grapes are picked between 21 and 24 percent in sugar content. The resulting wines average 12 percent alcohol by volume.

The alcohol produced by this process is called ethanol, or ethyl alcohol. There are many other commercial applications for ethanol. It can be utilized as an anti-freeze agent. It is unsurpassed as a rubbing alcohol and commonly sterilizes hospital instruments. It is a familiar component in tinctures and beauty aids. It can be an efficient source of combustion as it burns cleanly with intense heat—as you have undoubtedly noted with the brandy in Cherries Jubilee or Crepes Suzette.

With this process of fermentation creating a ready supply of wine alcohol, let us visualize the next step in the liquor chain called distillation. We place the fermented wine in a huge pot or tank and apply heat. Alcohol vaporizes at about 176 degrees Farenheit, a much lower temperature than the waters and grape solids in the wine. Water boils at 212 degrees Farenheit. The ethanol rises first as a steam and is captured and cooled in a series of copper condensing coils to produce a spirit or liquor, in this case called brandy—or distilled wine.

If we place this concentrated spirit back into another still and repeat the distilling process, we are re-distilling, and the second liquor produced will be purer than the first.

To put it another way, we eliminate more congeners, or grape particles, each time we distill a product.

Now, let's take a look at the proof, or percentage of alcohol in the liquor. Simply, the proof is twice the percentage of alcohol in the bottle. If we distilled the wine at 90 proof, we would produce forty-five percent alcohol by volume. The remaining fifty-five percent would be composed of the other wine fluids and solids. Through re-distilling the same wine to reach 190 proof, we would create a neutral liquor of 95 percent alcohol and only 5 percent of the other wine constituents, mainly water. In all distilling, then, the important decision is the proof at which the liquor is taken from the still.

If, instead of using grapes or fruits, we utilize grains as fermenting materials, we must take an intermediate step called malting. This is accomplished by steeping the grains in warm water until they sprout. This sprouting is called germination. Through germination, another enzymatic action, the grain starches are transformed into sugars. At this point, the material is called malt. It is placed in a mash tank with warm water where the sugars are extracted in what is then called sweet liquor, or a wort. Yeast is added to the wort and fermentation occurs just as it did with the natural fruit sugars in grapes, only now we have a beer. That's what beer is—fermented sugars from malted grains. Many people are happy to stop at this point and enjoy their beers and ales, but the distiller places his beer in a still to produce the stronger liquors.

Hence, brandy is distilled wine and bourbon is distilled beer.

In commercial distilling, the patent or continuous still has the very considerable advantage of handling a continuous flow of wine or beer at the rate of hundreds of gallons per hour. The pot still is limited to a single pot or batch at a time. Consequently, the continuous still is used almost universally in American liquor making, but some pungent pot still spirits are produced for blending purposes.

The next step in the liquor-making chain is aging. Usually, the concentrated alcohol is cut or diluted with distilled or demineralized water to a lower proof before storage in fifty gallon oak barrels in huge warehouses. The gentle harmonizing effects of oxidation in the barrels proceed to create a mellow, palatable drink from the fiery young distillate. Sometimes charcoal or wood chip filtering is utilized to accelerate the aging process. During the aging period, the most offensive of the congeners are either eliminated or softened. Most liquors require a minimum of two years in wood, with the top effective limit for most being eight years. However, we still find on the market some brandies and other liquors aged in wood up to 25 years.

Rectifying is next. This function is closely monitored and controlled by the federal government for it is at this point that federal taxes of $10.50 are paid on each proof gallon. Indeed, from the firing up of the still to the sealing of the storebound bottles, agents of the Bureau of Alcohol, Tobacco and Firearms are constant companions of the distiller.

Rectifying can include one or all of the following functions: blending of two different spirits such as a straight bourbon with neutral grain spirits; re-distillation of an already aged spirit to achieve an even lighter, more refined liquor; addition of coloring or flavoring agents, such as the caramel to provide a golden hue to liquor which is almost always naturally white; and, finally, re-distillation over flavoring agents such as herbs and botanicals in making gin. It is in rectification that the artisan becomes the artist. The master liquor blender is a supreme judge who can select a blend from literally thousands of tastes and smells in his aging cellars.

From the marriage of twenty to thirty of these separate liquors, he creates the distinctive blends on which brand success and continuity are based.

Depending upon the liquor, the new blend may have another period of aging before the final step of bottling for sale. At this point, more distilled water is added to reduce the liquor to the final bottle proof. A curious phenomenon occurs in that one gallon of water and one gallon of ethanol combine to make slightly less than two even gallons. The reason is that the smaller ethanol molecules slip comfortably between the larger water molecules. But never fear, with the government at hand, your every bottle contains the proper amount of alcohol.

And, there you have it. Those are the steps in creating the spiritous products which Raymond Lully so poetically described in the 13th century as . . . "The emanation of divinity destined to revive the energies of modern decreptitude."

A Mini Chronology on the Alcohols We Consume

Ancient Times to 500 AD

Paleozoic Era	Honey and grape wines ferment naturally as seas recede and bearing plants develop.
Paleolithic Era	During the Stone Age, nomads settle in permanent shelters, domesticate animals, and cultivate grains and fruits. Beer and wine are common to all ancient diets.
9750 B.C.	The cultivation of seeds, peas, beans and cucumbers is common. Pottery and weaving crafts appear, as does the consumption of alcohol during communal and religious rites.
5500	Farming in the Tigris-Euphrates river valleys near modern Iran is now common. This is the birthplace of the wine grapes of Western civilization.
2800	The Great Flood: Noah lands the ark at Mount Ararat and makes wines.
1200 to 800	The Phoenecians of Northern Africa became traders of the Mediterranean, and so further enrich culture and grape development.
600 to 247 (A.D.)	The Roman culture dominates Western civilization. Grapes arrive at Marseille in 600, and from 300 B.C. to 50 A.D. in the French areas of Burgundy,

	Bordeaux, the Loire Valley, and in Britain and the Rhine and Moselle river valleys of Germany.
4	Jesus is born.
2	Drinking feasts are common everywhere in Rome where three times as much wine is consumed as in Greece.
410	The Visigoths sack Rome.
475	The culturation and development of wine is now controlled by the monasteries of the church.

Medieval Times 500 to 1500 AD

550	St. Patrick brings Christianity to Ireland and probably the distilling techniques he learned in Alexandria.
563	St. Columba settles in Ionia Island off the coast of Scotland, forms an abbey, and is thought to have distilled the first Scotch whisky.
711 to 1492	Arabian Moors dominate Spain protecting vineyards for fruit, but wine abounds despite the prohibitions.
800	Jaber Ibn Hayyan (Geber), an Arabian alchemist, writes of "al Kohl" in *Liber Investigationes Magisteri*. The report covers the process of raising aqueous vapors: the freeing of liquor in the manner of a common eye cosmetic called "Kohl" which is made from antimony. Also, the Chinese distill spirits from rice wine.
822	Monks at Weser, Germany, use hops to preserve and flavor brews.
1000	The Vikings discover America and name it "Vinland" because of the profusion of wild grape vines there. Beer and mead is celebrated in the Anglo-Saxon epic "Beowulf."
1066	William, Duke of Normany, conquers England at Battle of Hastings. French-English wine trade rapidly expands

1150	White spirits from sweet fruit is distilled commonly as "alcool Blanc." Vodka, or neutral spirits, are first produced from grain in Russia, Poland, and Czechoslovakia.
1172	King Henry II invades Ireland and discovers a native spirit called "Uisge Baugh" which is made from native grains.
1250	Apothecaries in Italy commonly produce spirits spiced and sweetened as the earliest of liqueurs.
1290	Arnauld of Villeneuve, a professor of medicine at Montpellier in southern France, popularizes a medical panacea which he calls "aqua vitae" (the water of life). For the next 400 years, aqua vitae, in numerous forms, comprises a part of medical phamacopea. "It prolongs life, clears away ill humours, revives the heart, and maintains youth."
1411	The first French distilleries are given licenses in Alsace and Armagnac.
1419	The island of Madeira is settled by the Portugese and developed for agriculture including grape growing.
1451	German grain spirits called "schnapsteufel" (the devil's drink) are produced, the precurser of modern Schnapps.
1493	On his second expedition, Columbus takes sugar cane from the Canary Islands and plants at St. Croix in the Virgin Islands which begins the prodigious rum trade.

Early Modern Times 1500 to 1700 AD

1503	Scotland makes peace with England, opening the whiskey trade.
1510	The recipe for Benedictine liqueur is developed, but remains in private hands until 1884.
1525	Amaretto liqueur is developed in the town of Sarrona, Italy.

1553	Eau de vie de Cidre, or applejack, is first produced in Normandy, France. It is named Clavados in 1558 in honor of the Spanish Galleon visiting the area.
1561	Beer is first produced for sale in glass bottles in Germany.
1580	Jerez wine is commonly distilled to fortify and preserve Sherry.
1585	Dutch ships carry the first "burnt wine" or brandy from Cognac, France, to England and the Lowlands.
1606	The Virginia Company is formed, and early grape growing experiments begin.
1630	Governor John Winthrop makes the first prohibition move in an attempt to outlaw all liquor in Boston.
1640	Frances Sylvius, at the University of Leyden, Holland, develops a neutral aqua vitae from beer and adds juniper berry as a medicinal diuretic. For western civilization, this well-meaning procedure opened the causeway through which flowed the flood of grain spirits, a ubiquitous source for distillation. Frances named his concoction "Jenevre" which was shortened to Gin by the English.
1652	Spirits are made from corn and rye in the first commercial distillery in the United States, operated by William Kieft on Staten Island.
1657	Rum is first commercially produced in Massachusetts from West Indian molasses.
1680	Yeast is first viewed under a microscope by the Dutch scientist Van Leeuwenhoek.
1685	William Penn makes beer commercially in Philadelphia.
1690	Dom Perignon creates champagne in Epernay, France.
1693	William and Mary enact heavy duties to discourage French wine trade, and light duties to encourage Portuguese wine trade.

Late Modern Times 1700 to 1980

1733	Parliament passes the Molasses Act, raising tariffs on non-British molasses to the colonies.
1745	Rum becomes a staple on British navy ships as it is used to prevent scurvy.
1761	George Washington orders a copper still from England and sells spirits commercially the following year.
1769	The art of wine cultivation is brought to California from Mexico by Franciscan priest, Padre Junipero Serra — California's oldest industry is wine making.
1781	The cork is first used as a common stopper, a procedure which allows wine bottle aging.
1789	The Reverend Elijah Craig creates Bourbon from grain whiskey and limestone waters in Kentucky.
1791	The United States government first generates revenue by taxing whiskey and stills.
1808	The first formal Temperance Society in the United States is formed at the First Congregational Church in Saratoga, New York.
1818	Peter Smirnoff opens a vodka distillery in Moscow.
1833	The Supreme Court rules that states can regulate their liquor trade.
1837 to 1897	The blending of malt Scotch whiskey with the light spirits from the continuous still creates a vast new trade for product.
1843	Captain Sutter produces grape brandy for California gold miners.
1850	A new type of gin is developed in London without sweetener and aptly called London dry gin. Also, Dr. Johann Siegert begins exporting bitters from Angostura, Venezuela.
1852	Madeira wines celebrate their golden age in the United States.

1856	Under a commission of the wine industry, Louis Pasteur isolates yeast as the fermenting agent.
1860	Irish distillers begin to blend whiskey with neutral spirits in the manner of the Scotch blenders.
1862	The Bartender's Guide officially labels mixed drinks as cocktails.
1874	The Women's Christian Temperance Union is founded. Also, Prime Minister Gladstone loses his Parliament seat when he attempts to restrict gin consumption.
1876	Beer is first pasteurized for stability.
1880	An estimated eight percent of all Italian workers are involved in the wine industry.
1909	The Cognac areas become defined.
1916	Four hundred different individual brands of Irish whiskey are sold in the United States.
1920	On January 16, the 18th Amendment becomes the law of the land.
1929	The Police Commission of New York City estimates that there are 32,000 speak-easies and twice as many taverns as in pre-prohibition times. They estimate up to a total of 200,000 in the United States.
1933	On December 5, at 5:32 p.m. the 21st Amendment is passed, ending 13 years 10 months, and 18 days of legal prohibition.
1935	The first beer cans are sold in the United States, and over 700 brewers are involved in the business.
1972	American distillers are permitted to produce light whiskeys reminiscent of the Canadian types.
1978	Over four million cases of Tequila are sold, compared to a total of thirty thousand in 1960.
1980	Sales of Vodka by case is predicted to exceed forty million.

How to Choose The Right Spirit

THE AGE OF ALCOHOLIC INNOVATION EXPIRED WITH THE NINETEENTH CENTURY. ITS FINAL ACCOMPLISHMENT WAS THE APPLICATION OF THE SCOTTISH PRINCIPLE OF BLENDING TO KENTUCKY BOURBON AND PENNSYLVANIA RYE. BY 1900, ALL THE FORMS OF ALCOHOL NOW KNOWN HAD BEEN DISCOVERED, TRIED, AND APPRAISED. THE CHIEF CONCERN OF THE TWENTIETH CENTURY HAS BEEN TO APPRAISE THE NATURE OF ALCOHOL ITSELF.
—Berton Roueche'

The profusion of brand names and types needn't be all that confusing. Liquors, as other fluids we consume, sort out easily into the strong, forceful or assertive or into the light, mellow and often bland. Source materials and the level of alcohol or proof are the distinguishing elements. The following pages classify the major spirits available in the American market. Generally speaking, the lower the proof from the still, the stronger the taste of the spirit.

In historical perspective, the wild and woolly variations of quality of spirits in the nineteenth century gave way to two momentous government edicts. The first came in 1897 in the Bottled in Bond Act. The second occurred in 1909 when all types of distilled spirits were classified. Throughout the last century, hard liquor was sold in barrels and from hundreds of sources. Much was diluted with raw spirits or water. In times of excess, longer periods of aging in the wood produced mellower products. Hence, the idea of OLD as better took hold, and a few producers began to label their wares such as Old Forrester in 1870 and Old Grand Dad in 1872.

Bottling In Bond encouraged this individuality by assuring the customer of one hundred proof spirits of at least four years of age manufactured by one distiller. The green stamp at that time meant a badge of quality as compared to the uncertainty of open barrel spirits. The classifications in 1909 together with the development of new technology for efficient glass bottling assured both quality and identity by brands. The American spirit market bloomed into the advertising bonanza of today. Thousands of companies vie for your attention and dollar. Here are the broad outlines for your right choice!

CLASS	CHARACTERISTICS
Neutral Spirit	A distillate taken from the still above 190 proof and charcoal treated leaving no taste of original source material. 200 proof is pure alcohol. No character. Bland taste.
Vodka	The one truly neutral spirit as made for the American market. Some import vodkas have light tastes. The perfect base for cocktail mixes that do have tastes.
Whiskey	A bewildering array of choices. Mostly distinguished by character and taste due to distilling below 190 proof and with a particular mash source.
Bourbon Whiskey	Distilled from a minimum of 51% Corn at 160 proof or under and aged in new, charred white oak barrels for a minimum of two years. The oak char, the new barrels and low proof retain many congeners and much character.
Straight Whiskey	Unblended bourbon meeting proof, grain and aging requirements but usually produced at very low proof and aged much longer. Strong and Assertive. If preceded by words such as

	Wheat, Rye or Corn, the spirit is made from mash with a majority of those grains.
Blended Whiskey	Blends of usually 20 to 35% straight whiskey and grain neutral spirits and/or other agents such as sherry wine. Wide variations available in style and character with consistency the mark of the blender and the label. The objective in blended whiskey is uniform taste from bottle to bottle, year to year.
Tennessee Whiskey	Distillate with bourbon rules that is charcoal filtered immediately. Of great charm and character.
Sour Mash Whiskey	The mash contains about 25% of the residue of a previous mash for added character.
Canadian Whisky	No mistake. As in Scotland, they drop 'e' in the name. Canadians are all blends with corn the dominant mash together with rye, wheat and barley. With no requirement for new charred cooperage, the spirits are lighter and more mellow. As with Scotch, it is both bottled at home and shipped in bulk for American bottling.
Irish Whiskey	The only triple distilled spirit in the world, Irish whiskey is prepared from Irish grains and is sold nearly always as a blend. It is supremely light and mellow.
Blended Scotch Whisky	The majority of Scotch has been sold blended since the discovery of the continuous still and grain spirits in 1860s. The base for blending is malt whiskey prepared from pot stills containing characteristic peat smoke and taste. As with American blends individuality of style is prized with each label. Great variation exists but always the smoky

finish.

Single Malt Scotch	Rare but pungently attractive product of the original pot stills with no neutral grain spirits. Great character.
Rum	Distillate produced from by-products of sugar cane with wide variations in style from light Puerto Rican — taken at above 160 proof — to heavy Jamaican — taken often below 140 proof. As a rule of thumb, the white or silver labels are lighter with the gold or amber labels containing heavier spirit.
London Dry Gin	Distillate of nearly neutral spirit re-distilled over botanicals with juniper berries dominant. The proof of the base distillate contains some flavor and character identifiable in the bottle.
American Dry Gin	The distinction in American gin lies in the use of purely neutral spirits as the base. The redistillation over the botanicals produces no malt or whiskey character with a stronger juniper flavor.
Dutch Gin	Also called Hollands or Scheidam, Dutch Gin retains easily recognizable malt flavoring from the base whiskey. Like the single malt Scotch, Dutch Gin is strong and assertive.
Tequila	Tequila is a low proof, pot stilled distillate from the mash of the heart of the agave plant. Of great individuality and character, some Tequila is aged and in gold labeled bottles. Most is unaged and of light character.
Brandy	Brandy is the distillate of wine or the fermented mash of any fruit. If any fruit other than grapes is used, the bottle displays that fruit name. Brandies are made throughout the world in a bewildering array of styles.

Cognac	The popular import brandy derives from a very limited area in Southern France and is produced by double distilling in pot stills and taken at very low proof. While 90 percent is sold at the Three Star level at an average of four years in aging, most cognacs rank among the most pungent and powerful of spirits.

Armagnac	A product of Southern France, Armagnac is double distilled in combination pot-continuous stills, aged in local wood and emerges a slightly harder, cleaner spirit than cognac.

American Brandy	Much greater proportions of continuous still distillate are utilized in producing the lighter, often sweeter American style brandy. For this reason, it is often used as a cocktail base as well as a sipping drink.

Since there is no accounting for taste, it is advisable to first experiment with the world of spirits at a local pub. You can determine the pronounced differences between single malt and blended Scotch brands, as well as the range between the many blends by contrasting them in shot glasses. Order two types with a water back, and carefully smell before tasting each. Over several months of personal taste testing, you can develop great facility and confidence.

Basic Definitions You Will Need

DRINK! FOR YOU KNOW NOT WHENCE YOU CAME, NOR WHY. DRINK! FOR YOU KNOW NOT WHY YOU GO, NO WHERE!
—Omar Khayyam

WINE IS THE MOST HEALTHFUL AND HYGIENIC OF ALL BEVERAGES.
—Louis Pasteur

ALCOHOL The alcohol to remember is ethyl alcohol, also known as ethanol, a by-product of the fermentation of sugars. A number of lesser alcohols also are created in fermentation in minute quantities, but *ethyl* is the *beverage alcohol*.

FERMENTATION Fermentation is a form of combustion which re-aligns each molecule of sugar (carbon, hydrogen and oxygen) creating from each, two new molecules each of ethyl alcohol and carbon dioxide. This is the natural process discovered by ancient man by which fruit becomes wine and germinated grain becomes beer. The process is caused by yeasts which operate under the surface of the grape juice without benefit of air—hence the fermentation is anaerobic.

A STILL A still is a container or device used to vaporize and to capture alcoholic spirits.

A POT STILL The pot still is the oldest, simplest mechanism used in distilling. It is akin to a pot on a stove with an inverted funnel used to catch the alcoholic vapors and a cooling chamber so that the steam can return to a fluid. The pot still cooks one batch of wine or beer at a time. When fully distilled a new batch is placed in the pot.

PATENT OR CONTINUOUS STILL Invented in 1832 by an Irishman with the unlikely name of *Coffey*, a continuous still is simply an ingenious series of pot stills stacked one upon the other, allowing the capturing of vapors or spirits at various levels or proofs. The considerable advantage is that it can handle a continuous supply of wine or beer all day long—hundreds of gallons an hour. This tremendous efficiency factor is the reason that the majority of the world's liquors are made in continuous stills.

MALT OR MALTED GRAIN While the sugars in wine ferment naturally, grain is composed of starch which will not ferment. Hence, malting or the germinating of barley, corn or rye grain is a necessary first step before fermentation. The grain is placed in a bath of warm water. When the grain sprouts, the starch saccharifies, or changes to sugar. This is called malting. The malted grain is then ground and mixed with water and yeast for fermentation.

CONGENER Understand the congener and you will identify the tastes and the character of various liquors. Congeners are elements passed over from the original wine or beer, such as mineral salts, aldehydes, acetic acid, esters and fusel oils or new compounds created in fermentation and distillation. In sum, congeners provide the recognizable spirit tastes and aromas. In heavy concentration, they are often unpleasant, even repulsive. In balance, they delight the senses. Esters are combinations of acids, alcohols and oxygen which create the distinctive fruity aromas as well as the bouquet in aged wines.

FUSEL OILS These congeners are pungent, even nauseous, higher alcohols often called heads or foreshots since they vaporize first in a still at lower heat levels. They precede the true ethyl alcohol vapors which are called middle liquors in distillation.

ALDEHYDES These congeners are volatile fluids created by the oxidation of alcohols and they pass over last in the distillation process at the highest temperatures. Hence, they are termed tails of feints. As with esters, they are important to the bouquet or smell of the liquor.

OXIDATION Oxidation is the chemical process by which wine and all spirits eventually decompose. Think of an apple turning brown when exposed to the air and you visualize oxidation. It is, therefore, the fatal enemy of wine, or any other fruit for that matter. By contrast, it is the gentle harmonizer, the mellowing agent for the harsh new liquors. They mellow by oxidation as they rest year after year in the aging barrels. Finally, within our own bodies, ethyl alcohol is oxidized freeing the calories as energy.

PROOF Though the British still use the exact odd percentages, in America, proof is registered as exactly twice the percent of ethyl alcohol in the bottle. A shot of 100 proof vodka is composed of fifty percent ethyl alcohol and fifty percent distilled water. An eighty proof brandy has forty percent ethyl alcohol in the bottle.

PROOF OFF THE STILL The liquors taken directly from the still before being cut or diluted with distilled or demineralized water also are measured in proof. Again, the proof is twice the actual amount of ethyl alcohol in the fluid. The remaining fluid, of course, is constituted of the wine or beer being distilled. An absolutely pure spirit would be all ethyl alcohol without a single trace of wine or beer. So, the proof from the still tells you the percentage of alcohol in the spirit. A liquor taken from the still at 130 proof is constituted of sixty-five percent ethanol and thirty-five percent of the wine or beer from which it was distilled. It has a very high congener count. Obviously, an absolutely pure spirit would be taken from the still at 200 proof. It would be one hundred percent ethanol and nothing else. Thus—a neutral spirit.

NEUTRAL SPIRIT Neutral (formerly called cologne) spirits are those taken from the still at such a high proof that they are colorless and nearly odorless, utterly lacking in congeneric character.

BLENDING This is simply the marrying of two or more liquors or other palatable substances. Consistency is the primary aim of the blender in order that your favorite scotch or cabernet wine tastes the same each time you purchase it.

IN BOND Literally, in bond signifies federal control over the liquor. When referring to whiskey, bottled-in-bond means the product is a straight whiskey, at least four years old, which had been bottled at 100 proof. That's really all it means. It may be superb or quite common whiskey, as the designation has no relation to the quality.

DRY Our final essential term is dry, and it is perhaps the most confusing since it has a number of meanings in alcoholic beverages. As example, dry means a lack of sugar to the winemaker. A medium-sweet wine has a definite sweet overtone. By contrast, a dry gin is one made without a trace of the grain congeners. Dry gin is distilled a second time with herbs and a neutral spirit. Even more confusing, a dry martini is that same dry gin served with but a hint of dry vermouth which itself has some sugar in it. Confused? Oh, well, keep in mind that most often dryness is the absence of sugar in wine.

These are the essential working definitions. They are used repeatedly in the features which follow.

Wine and Liquor
The abc's

a

What is Absinthe?

In the naughty Paris of 1890, the Cocktail hour was called *l'heure verte* or the green hour in honor of Absinthe. The liqueur made from heavy infusions of wormwood (artemesia absinthium) anise, spinach nettles and herbs is now banned since it was feared to drive people mad. Pernod with heavy anise flavor is its successor!

What is Advocaat?

One of the earliest home prepared drinks in Holland is Advocaat, an egg nog type liqueur. Now bottled for public sale, it is made by heating to the point of thickening or emulsifying eggs and brandy. Sometimes a light touch of fennel or maraschine is added. It's a delight!

What is Aftertaste?

A critical step in judging wines and liquors is found in the lingering presence in the throat *after swallowing*. It can range from a gentle fragrance to unpleasant burning. The mouth and throat warm the fluids on the way through releasing brand new tastes and smells.

What is Aguardiente?

A strict construction of the word would mean "water of the famished." This is but one of the many variations of the original theme of aqua vitae or water of life. The Spanish speaking call many liquors by this name whether from grain, grape or cane sugar.

How is Beer Alcohol Measured?

The handy hydrometer is used to calculate the specific gravity of the beer wort before and after fermentation. Calculations then yield the percent of alcohol BY WEIGHT. This contrasts with the percentage of alcohol BY VOLUME used in most beverage alcohols.

What is A Beverage Alcohol?

Wine, beer and honey wine called mead have been consumed in nearly all countries and through all times. Refinements of fermenting and distilling have created a bewildering array of potables which combine ethyl alcohol with every form of pleasant flavoring. Any liquid with more than one half a percent of ethyl alcohol is termed a beverage alcohol and thus subject to federal taxes.

Does Alcohol Raise Body Temperature?

To the surprise and dismay of many, alocholic drinks actually lower body temperatures. A person feels warmer as heat escapes through the skin pores. In fact, rum, popular in warm climates, cools more than ice water!

What is Denatured Alcohol?

Ethyl alcohol is denatured by adding nauseating, poisonous substances such as formaldehyde, kerosene, gasoline, shellac and pine tar. It is then a jack-of-all-trades used in everything from shampoo to embalming fluid.

What is Wood Alcohol?

As contrasted with what we drink, the denatured type is composed of lethal methyl alcohol. Originally fermented from wood, it is made today of carbon monoxide and hydrogen. It is used in commercial products such as shellac and solvents. Blindness and death can result from human consumption. Beware!

What is Ale?

Ale is a type of beer—a distinctive malt beverage which is brewed at higher temperature with a unique variety of yeast that rises to the top of the fermenter. Always with a pronounced hop flavor, ale often is higher in alcohol and is bitter-sweet to the taste.

What is an Alembic?

The alembic is the pot still used to make cognac in Southern France. Over four thousand of these simple devices are in use. They consist of a boiler, a head for the wine, a copper coil condenser and the receiving barrel. The rich, flavorful pungency of cognac comes from these simple country stills.

What is Al Kohl?

AL KOHL, known to us as alcohol, is attributed to an Arabian alchemist in the year 800 who developed distilling from native brews. Since the magic was accomplished by vaporizing in the same manner as a popular cosmetic eye paint called KOHL, he dubbed it Al Kohl or like kohl.

What is Alsatian wine?

A seventy mile strip of land in Alsace has produced fine wines for thousands of years. The Roman soldiers farmed these producing vineyards. Alsatian wines are nearly always white and made from the riesling grapes popular in neighboring Germany. Unlike the rest of France, the grape varieties are on the label.

What is Amaretto?

The newly popular cocktail — THE GODFATHER — owes its piquant, smooth taste to a 56 proof liqueur made from apricot pulp and kernels. Called Amaretto, appreciated for over 400 years in its native Italy. Just mix it with scotch or bourbon. Atsa Vera nize!

What is Amontillado?

Come to know the treasure of Spain, Amontillado. The fine dry sherries are classified as Fino. The darkest and fullest of these unique blends are shipped throughout the world as Amontillado. Over ice or in a snifter, Amontillado delivers the nutty, fragrant unparalleled aperitif.

What is an Amphora?

The graceful, tapering egg-shaped vase popular in ancient Greece was the amphora. An important use of the vessel was the aging of wine. Thus, the Greeks were the first civilized people to know the glories of matured wines!

What is Angelica?

Aside from Zinfandel in the table wines, California can claim a unique wine in Angelica. The concoction is simplicity itself. Pure brandy is blended into fresh grape juice producing by far the sweetest of all drinks. While primarily a cheap, popular wine, there are now a few premium quality brands on the market.

What is Anisette?

Hippocrates loved his anisum. The Frenchman and Spaniard of today treasure their soothing after dinner drinks made from the common pimpinella anisum and a dozen or so other milder herbs and seeds. Licorice-like anisette is very sweet, low in alcohol and provides a nice finish to a meal.

What is Anisone?

Perhaps the most popular taste in liqueurs is the exquisite, tangy-sweet anise seed. A popular flavor also in breads and puddings, anise is the base for Anisette, one of the sweetest cordials produced around the world. The Italian version called Anisone is typically higher in alcohol and lower in sugar. Bella, Bellisimo!

What is an Aperitif?

From the Latin *operio* which means *to open*, the appetizer is the light medium dry wine designed to stimulate the appetite before the meal. Often containing quinine and other scented herbs, aromatized wines are vermouths, dry sherries and secret recipes like Dubonnet and Lillet.

How Old are Aperitifs?

Aperitifs date from most ancient times. Greek herbalists were fond of soaking their ritual concoctions in wines to make them more palatable—and probably more effective! Fruits, flavoring agents, seeds, flowers and herbs were used. Vermouth became the first commercial aperitif in the late 18th century. Ranging from dry to semi-sweet, aperitifs sharpen the appetite and therefore are correctly used before the meal.

What is Appellation Contrôlée?

French winemakers began to submit to a system of controls in 1855. This highly ordered, strictly classified program is designed to assure a level of quality control in the top ten percent of French produced wines. Rigid control is exercised over types of grapes, amount produced and geographic origin. Look for the words on the label!

What are Appetizer Wines?

Appetizer equals aperitif! Both refer to the light, aromatic wines designed to stimulate the appetite before the meal. Ranging from very dry to moderately sweet, they include the sherries, the vermouths, Madeira and even flavored Marsalas. To your health!

What is Aquavit?

Aquavit, akvavit, akevit in Scandanavia or Schnapps in Germany all are in a family of pure, white native spirits quite often distilled from potatoes. In both sweet and dry fiery versions, aquavit is commonly flavored with carraway seed and cummin. Try it, like the Swedes, chilled with smorgasbord!

What is Aqua Vitae?

The Spanish alchemist Arnold of Vila Nova first ascribed medicinal qualities to distilled spirits around 1260. He called them Water Of Life and grandly praised their restorative powers. In other languages from Gaelic to French the theme recurred — Eau de vie, Uisege Baugh — waters of a better life!

What is Arrack?

One of the common terms for liquor in Asia is arrack, often spelled araka, arraki, arak or raki. From Greece through the Middle East, it encompasses liquors made from everything from palm sap to cane sugar rum. Enjoy it on your tour with boiled eggs and cheese!

What is Batavia Arak?

One of the delights of the rum trade is Batavia Arak made from molasses in Java, East Indies. A special wild yeast and local rice are added to the fermenting tubs. The rum is aged in Java four years, then shipped to Holland for more ageing and bottling. A light, quaint, delightful rum!

What is Armagnac?

The grape brandy produced in the district of Gers in Southern France lays exclusive claim to the name Armagnac. It is said to possess a drier, harder taste than Cognac derived from the hard, black oak of Gascony in which it is aged.

What is Asbach Uralt?

While most German brandies are of inferior quality, Asbach Uralt is treasured throughout the western world. The key to quality in this Rudesheim distillery is the wine which is imported from the Cognac and Armagnac regions of France. Light, mellow German brandy from French wines is aged in French Limousin wood. A cooperative delight!

What is Astringency? a,b

Astringency is often confused with bitterness. They go together often but are quite distinct. The phenolic compounds from the skins in red wines cause both sensations. Bitterness is one of the four true tastes, while astringency is a feeling created by the puckering in the mouth. Astringency accompanies pronounced bitterness!

What is Auslese?

The German winemaker specializes in selective late picking as the grapes develop increasing concentrations of grape sugar. The word Auslese means selected. It is the second of four stages of late harvesting and always produces a markedly sweet wine.

Who was Bacchus?

Bacchus was one of the more famed gods of mythology who's responsibility was fertility in nature. Great feasts and celebrations called Bacchanalia were held in his honor in both Athens and Rome. A son of Zeus, Bacchus spread the wine culture throughout western civilization. Here's a salute to wise old Bacchus!

What is Bamberger Rauchbier?

In long gone days, the home brewer dried his brewing malt in the simplest way possible — over an open fire. The smoke imparted strong and acrid tastes similar to Scotch whiskey made from peat smoked malt. This tradition of beechwood log smoked malt is continued today in the small town of Bamberg, West Germany. For a *really different* beer, look for Bamberger Rauchbier.

What is Beaujolais?

A variety of wine developing great new popularity is the mellow, fruity, young Beaujolais. In its native area south of the great Burgundies, the Gamay grape matures early and, unlike most reds, needs little aging. It's a good beginner red!

What is Premieur Beaujolais?

At midnight plus one minute, on November 15th, French wine law allows the first release of the delightful young red wine called Beaujolais. This first blush is scarcely a month in aging and is light and delightfully fruity. Another month will pass before the full vintage may be released for sale!

What is a Beer Adjunct?

Over the years, Americans have expressed their preference for the light, pale and stable beers. These desirable flavors and cl..ster are obtained by a delicate balance of additives such as cracked corn, rice, grits, honey and even popular corn flakes!

What is a Beer Barrel?

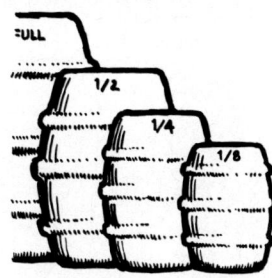

Americans are rolling out the beer barrel in numbers, but they probably would be surprised at their odd gallonages. The pitch-lined wood barrel of old has been replaced by stainless steel or aluminum. The full barrel contains exactly thirty one gallons while the picnic or pony barrel has exactly 3.875 bubbly gallons!

What is Bock Beer?

Perhaps the oldest of old wives' liquor tales, handed down faithfully from one generation to the next, is that which has bock beer being brewed from the sediment of barrels cleaned in springtime. It is, rather, a special heavy and often sweeter brew usually created as a herald to approaching springtime. The name comes from Einbeck, Germany from which huge quantities of fine beer were exported in the Middle Ages.

What is Dark Beer?

In dark, stout and porter, the malt or germinated barley is carmelized by roasting to produce color, "burnt" taste and fuller body. Addition of more hops produces bitterness. Porter gets a dash of licorice.

What is Dehydrated Beer?

Believe it or not—for brewer's use only—man has dehydrated even beer! Fresh beer is flash frozen creating ice crystals of about three quarters of the volume. When these snow flakes are skimmed off, you have really dry beer concentrated for ease in shipping.

b ## What is Distiller's Beer?

To understand nearly all liquors, you must comprehend what is termed wash or distiller's beer. The fermentation of grain mash produces this simple beer. It lacks the hop flavoring and cereal adjuncts of commercial beers. It is distilled directly into whiskey or re-distilled into vodka.

What is Draught Beer?

Draught (pronounced DRAFT) or tap beer is packaged in aluminum barrels at the brewery. It is the oldest and still the most popular beer, a fresh, unpasteurized brew normally consumed within a week of brewing. Have another schooner!

What is Flavor in Beer?

True beer lovers decry the increasing softness in American beer. Beer flavor is a complex consequence of the constituents including carbohydrates, sugars, enzymes, vitamins, minerals and principally hops (a relative of the mulberry). Unfortunately, brewers use half the hops of 1935!

What is Beer Foam?

Universally beloved, the froth on your brew denotes quality in the product. Residue bubbles of the carbon dioxide gas created in fermentation burst to the top of the glass carrying with them a network of proteins. Abundant beer foam aids in digestion, adds piquancy by tickling the tongue and renders good taste. Here's to the head!

What are Beer Grains?

The abundant earth produces grain starches in many forms. Since all are fermentable following germination into sugars, brews have been a common source of beverage alcohol. By far the best of the bunch is barley, near universal in beer making. Africans use the more abundant millet and Japanese prefer rice for Sake beer. American brewers often blend corn and rice for paler color and snappier taste!

What is Kraeusened Beer?

In a system very much akin to the second fermentation in producing sparkling wines, the Kraeusening tank encloses already finished and aged beer with a dose of newly fermenting wort. The resulting carbon dioxide bubbles are bound by nature in the beer adding to the flavor and aroma.

What is Lager Beer?

A lagern in German is a storage area. Hence, to lager is to store or age a new brew. This period of cold aging causes a mellowing and maturing of a lively new brew. Nearly all beer you consume is lager unless it is named as ale, malt liquor, or stout or porter. Lager beer is usually light and satisfying!

What is Beer Life?

Unlike most foods we consume from can or bottle, our beloved brew has a predictably limited life. Even the unpasteurized brew placed in the draught barrels must be consumed within thirty days. Pasteurized bottled and canned beer last no more than three months. Enjoy your brew young, fresh and bubbly!

What is Light Beer?

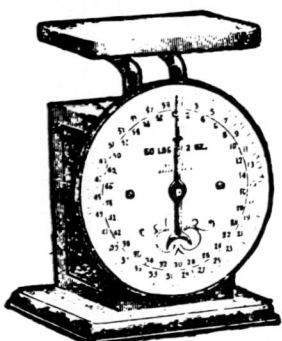

In brewing, much of original barley grain starch remains in beer as dextrine, a tasteless carbohydrate. By eliminating dextrine, beer calories drop from about 136 to about 90 per bottle. VOILA, LIGHT CALORY BEER!

What is Near Beer?

It took that determined woman Carrie Nation and her familiar axe to reduce the brew of ancient times to its cereal level. During prohibition, the alcohol was distilled or cooked out of perfectly good beer reducing it to liquid breakfast food—thus called near Beer!

What is Beer Pasteurizing?

Canned and bottled brew is stabilized much as milk by the process of pasteurization. Once bottled, it is shuttled slowly through a chamber in which heat is gradually applied and removed. The active yeast and bacteria alike are destroyed.

What is Weiss beer?

A popular variation of the ever popular brew in Germany is Weissbrau. Literally, the word means white and the lightness comes from using wheat as the grain instead of barley. High in carbon dioxide, it foams liberally and happily in the glass.

What is Benedictine, D.O.M.?

Benedictine is a world famous, richly sweet plant liqueur. First made in 1510 as a medicinal nostrum by monks, it utilizes many seeds and herbs with cognac as the liquor. D.O.M. on the label means TO GOD, MOST GOOD, MOST GREAT.

What is Beverage Consumption?

It will come as no surprise that Americans have chosen soda pop their favorite beverage — at thirty four gallons per person each year. Other close favorites are coffee at thirty two, milk at twenty four and beer at twenty one gallons. Meteoric wine, the least consumed at slightly under two gallons, has doubled in the last decade and will soon bypass distilled spirits. Wine is on its way!

What Are Bitters?

Without doubt, bitters are the least recognized of alcoholic beverages. A type of cordial, bitters are now used primarily to flavor mixed drinks, though they once were stomach balms. Highly aromatic seeds, barks or roots are soaked in spirits to release the unique flavors found in your favorite cocktail.

What is the Black Rooster Legend?

The Political League of Chianti has used the Gallo Nero—black rooster—as a symbol since 1200. Legend says the borderline between Florence and Siena was settled by having two men walk until they met at the crack of dawn. The wily Florentines chose an ill fed scrawny black rooster which woke their man first thereby gaining the most territory!

What is Blanc de Blanc?

This phrase in French is translated *white on white*. In practice, it refers to a small amount of French Champagne produced from the white skinned chardonnay grape exclusively. It is a lighter and more expensive cuvee. The vast bulk of Champagne is produced from red grapes with a bit of Chardonnay for style.

What is Blanc de Noir?

It is a surprise to some that French Champagne, nearly always white, is produced from black skinned grapes. The fresh grapes are carefully picked over to eliminate imperfect fruit and gently pressed to release the white pulp for fermentation. Hence *Blanc de Noir* or, white wine from black grapes!

What is a Bocksbeutel?

A favorite canteen of the early German housewife was made from leather in the shape of an organ of a goat. By the middle of the 18th Century, the familiar pouch was designed in glass. Today it contains the famous green-eyed gold Steinwein from Germany as well as the popular Rose types from Portugal.

What is a Bodega?

Bodega is Spanish for storehouse. Far from prosaic store rooms, the bodega for aging Spanish sherry is more akin to a cathedral with its vaulting roof line and stunning white exterior. Fine sherries are born, age and mature for hundreds of years in these wine churches!

What Was a Bootlegger?

Far from the romantic image, a true bootlegger was a small, pint-sized flask in common use during the stage coach era. The small bottle could be filled at each tavern stop and conveniently carried in the high boots of the time.

What is Bordeaux Wine?

The greatest wines of France — perhaps of the world — originate in the small area surrounding the town of Bordeaux. The Roman Pliny complimented fine wines from the area as early as the first century. Nearly thirty million cases are produced annually, with the rich red Cabernet Sauvignon and luscious sweet Sauternes dominant. For the best, look for the chateau botting — mis en bouteille au chateau — for the very best!

What is Bourbon?

Bourbon is a distinctive robust beverage alcohol first distilled by Rev. Elijah Craig in Bourbon County, Kentucky. Bourbon must be distilled from a mash of 51 percent or more of corn and it cannot be taken above 160 proof to ensure a strong congeneric flavor. Aging in new charred oak barrels lends another important taste to America's unique drink!

What is Brandewijn?

A precious cargo in the Middle Ages from southern France to Holland was marked BRANDEWIJN. At this time, an enterprising sea captain boiled out or concentrated the wine intending to add water again at his destination. His customers preferred the distilled spirit called BRAND or burnt wine, a word anglicized to BRANDY.

b

What is Brandy?

Brandy is liquor from distilling of wine or fermented fruit mash. Wine brandy is aged in wood and may be savored straight or mixed in any cocktail. Cognac is French wine brandy from Charente-Maritimes Provinces.

What is Napoleon Brandy?

Don't be confused! If someone offers you a nineteenth century Napoleon Brandy, watch your purse. No liquor ages once bottled except wine. However some fine contemporary Napoleon labeled cognacs are produced that see up to twenty years aging in wood before bottling. Buy the latter with confidence and expectation. Shun the former!

What is Pot Still Brandy?

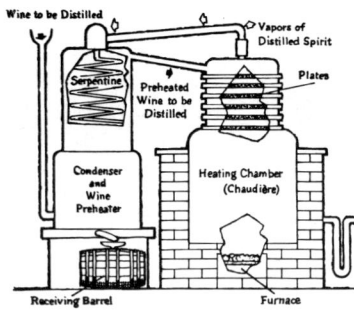

Blindfolded, anyone can easily pick the pungent bouquet and the commanding tastes of European brandy and cognac. The ancient pot still is the cause of the distinction in the spirit. Simplicity itself, the all copper pot still allows the retention of the strong congeners — heads and tails — which impart flavor and rich aromas.

What is a Bucket of Suds?

Not so many years ago, the majority of beer sold came from wooden barrels as draught beer. It was necessary to send a container to the corner tavern to get beer. A practice grew of larding the sides of the pail to prevent the precious cargo from foaming. Hence, the bucket still had its *suds*.

What are Calories in Wine?

Dry table wines [those without sugar] average 25 calories per ounce—about 100 calories in a four ounce serving. That compares to about 160 calories in a full glass of milk. Of course, sweet dessert wines have up to 45 calories per ounce!

What is Calvados?

Calvados is named from the Normandy town in northern France where it is made by distilling the cider of fine, ripe apples. In America, we call the product Apple-Jack. However, the Normans pot-distill their cider and age it up to ten years in wood making incomparable apple brandy — CALVADOS!

What is Chablis?

The most distinctive of all white wines is Chablis. True Chablis from the region in Northern France is the most delicate, flinty dry wine of all — the perfect companion of a fish entree. Produced exclusively from the Chardonnay in France, it is imitated world wide and made in many softer, sweet blends. True Chablis, wherever made, is dry and tart!

What is Champagne Sugar Level?

Don't let the bubbles fool your taste buds. All sparkling wines contain a dose of sugar added before bottling. A very few French champagnes called Nature are produced without sugar. The sugars by volume in champagnes are: BRUT up to 1 percent; EXTRA DRY up to 3 percent; SEC up to 4 percent; and the real sweet bubbly DOUX and COLD DUCK up to 10 percent.

C

What is Champagne Tax?

Alas, to the dismay of all true lovers of the bubbly, the federal government grimly holds to its nearly confiscatory champagne tax levied during the second World War. At $3.40 per gallon, the tax is twenty times that of still wine!

What is Charmat Champagne?

Traditional champagne is produced by a second fermentation in each and every bottle. In 1910 a French winemaker named Eugene Charmat simplified the process by using a 500 gallon steel tank for the second fermentation. Called bulk process on the bottle, Charmat champagne is as good as the wine from which it is made!

What is Vintage Champagne?

The afficionado of vintaged French wines is quite happy to purchase authentic unvintaged champagne. Unlike other classified wines, most champagne is blended from several years and up to forty different wines. Perhaps twice each decade, the harvest is of such superb quality that a vintage champagne is made—a light, delicate and quite expensive bottling!

What is Chaptilization?

In Germany and Northern France, there are often cloudy spells during grape ripening seasons. When this occurs, the fruit lacks sufficient sugar to produce the common twelve percent alcohol wines. Cane sugar is added to produce the alcohol, a practice forbidden in California.

What is Chartreuse?

The only liqueur of commercial importance still under the jurisdiction of a religious order is the popular Chartreuse. Produced since 1607 in France and Spain, this sweet concoction is said to contain up to 140 herbs, plants and spices in a super-secret formula. Green Chartreuse is sold at 100 proof and lighter yellow at 86 proof. Try this brandy based cordial to finish a perfect evening.

What is a Chevalier du Tastevin?

Of all the variety of wine appreciation societies of the world, the 17,000 member Chevaliers are at least the most handsomely costumed if not the most prestigious. Formed in 1934 to promote French Burgundy wines, the group is headquartered in the imposing 600 year old Chateau du Clos de Vougeot. Great and elaborate feasts are staged in the hall with the members arrayed in striking medieval costumes.

What is Chateauneuf du Pape

C

The Greeks are credited with planting vines along the Rhone river in Southern France as early as 500 AD. In the Fourteenth Century, the Catholic Popes lived in Avignon and developed vineyards which still produce great wines. These blends of up to thirteen varieties of grapes are big, full bodied and noble reds.

What is Chianti?

True Chianti is made only in Central Italy in the Tuscany Province. Grapes used include the Sangiovese, Canaiolo, Trebbiano, and Malvasia del Chianti. All others are sham and imposters! A secondary fermentation (called governo) induced by raisoned grapes produces the rich color and matchless taste!

C

What is Chieu?

It is a surprise to some to learn that the Chinese record wine making more than four thousand years ago. Chieu or Chiew is their all purpose word meaning wine, liquor, brew or liqueur. Persian grape vines were introduced at the time of Christ, but most Chinese "wine" is really brew made from rice and millet seeds.

What is a Cock and Bull Story?

The telling of tall tales has never been easier under the gentle persuasion of a friendly libation. The Cock and Bull tavern in ancient England was particularly noted as a ribald inn, a place where loose tongues weaved tales of valor and accomplishment. Hence outlandish braggadocio became identified as Cock and Bull!

When was Cognac First Aged?

When the Dutchman, William of Orange, assumed the throne of England, an alliance with Spain began which blocked wine and brandy trade from 1701 to 1714. Cognac makers were forced to store their spirits in barrels from local oak trees. When trade was resumed, the cognac was found to be improved by the aging!

What is Five Star Cognac?

Cognac is that brandy produced and aged in the Charente Province in Southeastern France. No other brandy throughout the world can be Cognac. The stars on the bottles denote relative quality in terms of wood aging before bottling. Three stars means 3 to 5 year old brandy. The best is five stars meaning seven or more years of age!

What is Cointreau?

Probably the world's best known and loved liqueur is named after its founders Adolphe and Edouard Cointreau. Made since 1849 in the Loire Valley, there are now 13 plants worldwide producing the light and sweet, 80 proof cordial from sweet and bitter orange peels.

What is Cold Duck?

Produced from a mixture of white and red sparkling wines, cold duck has the highest sugar content of any bubbly wine. Its unique name came about from the corruption of the German words Kalte Ende—meaning the cold end of the evening when all remaining wines were mixed in a toast. A misplaced T created Kalte Ente or Cold Duck!

What is the Color in Liquors?

All distilled liquors are light or white in color, the fewer the congeners the lighter the distillate. Aging in charred oak barrels lends a golden hue to bourbons. The addition of a small amount of caramel syrup at the time of rectification creates the pleasing hue in rum, brandy, whiskey and even some tequilas!

What is Commandaria?

The world's oldest named wine is luscious, sweet Commandaria from the forbidding isle of Cyprus. Named by the Knights Templar in the 12th Century, it is made by farmers who ferment and age it in pitch lined jars up to a year. It is a tangy, earthy dessert delight!

C

What is Cream of Tartar?

Aside from the wine itself, fermentation creates a number of useful by-products. None exceeds the ultimate uses of the dominant fruit acid of the grape—*tartaric acid*. Tartar is obtained from the spent husks and pomace and is used in baking powder, in the form of salts for photography and in the form of acid for flavoring. Another wonder of the grape!

What is a Creme?

Literally, creme means cream! Hence, logically, cremes are the very rich, fruity, creamy and oh-so-sweet cordials which are perfect as dessert toppings. Often low in alcohol, cremes are used in crushed ice as frappe desserts.

What is a Congener?

If you understand the role of the congener, you will easily appreciate the differences and likenesses in the range of liquors. Congeners are traces of oils, esters and acids passed over the fermentation and distillation of liquors. The lower the proof, the more the congeners. In sum, they are the taste and aroma characteristics that distinguish one type from another.

What is a Cordial?

In Latin *cordis* means heart. According to Heronymous Braunschweig, published in 1520, the earliest use of cordials or liqueurs was to stimulate the heart and lighten the spirit. The beverages were compounded of liquors and sweeteners to make palatable the often bitter medicines. Those doctors had heart!

What is the Cote de Nuits?

One can hardly conjure in the imagination a twelve mile strip of the earth's crust of the significance of the Cote de Nuits. From the town of Fixin on the North to Nuit St. George on the South, the Pinot Noir grape produces the ultimate in burgundy wines. One can be *sure* with Gevrey-Chambertin, Vosne-Romanee and Vougeot!

What is a Criadera?

The enterprising Spanish long ago developed an aging system in which wines from each new year were blended thoroughly to produce the magnificent sherries. The uppermost barrels are all called criadera — or nurseries. Passing down each year, the bottlings are taken from the bottom barrels called the solera. Thereby the Spanish Sherry you drink could have some molecules hundreds of years old!

What is a Cru?

Don't be confused by the French designations Crû and Crû classé. A cru is literaly a growth or an agricultural yield from a plot of land. Therefore a good cru is a great growth. However, when shown on a label from the Bordeaux growing region with the word classe, the phrase means a specific classified vineyard.

What is Curacao?

Oranges are a gift of the Orient that found delightful acceptance in Middle Ages in Europe. Curacao is a romantic island of the Indies noted for a particularly bitter orange. In making these fine liqueurs such as Curacao and Cointreau, only the peel is used for its aromatic oil. The liqueur is wonderfully bitter-sweet.

c,d

What is a Cuvée?

In French, cuve means a cask or vat. By doubling the consonant at the end, we refer to a specific batch or blend of wine. The same term often appears on American labels signifying a certain batch of wine made at one time. It is often reserved for the very best quality bottlings.

What is Degorgement?

The French or traditional method of champagne making requires the secondary fermentation to take place right in the bottle. A skilled artisan is needed to disgorge the resulting sediment from the neck of the bottle. The material is frozen in brine and popped out like an ice-cream bar! Wine with sugar is then added and the bottle is recorked for sale.

What is a Degree Day?

In grape growing, the degree days are a summation of the daily temperatures ranging above 50 degrees Fahrenheit. The vine does not mature below that level. The average degree days determine the type of grapes to be planted.

What is Denominazione Di Origine Controllata?

VINO
BARBARESCO
DENOMINAZIONE D'ORIGINE CONTROLLATA
'N ZONA DI ORIGINE DALLA ANTICA CASA VITIVINICOLA
i MINUTO - Produttori -
BARBARESCO - (PIEMONTE)

In imitation of the French system of quality control, the Italian government established in 1963 their CONTROLLED DENOMINATION OF ORIGIN. Strict standards of grape production and wine making are imposed on those special wines. There are three levels: SEMPLICE for ordinary wines; CONTROLLATA for wines under special controls and GARANTITA for the finest Italian wine.

What is the Deutsche Weinstrasse?

The German Wine Road meanders along the Rhine River from Bockenheim to the Wine Gate at Schwigen on the Alsace frontier. With the Haardt Mountains as backdrop, this strip encompasses some of the most beautiful scenery in the Western world. It also includes the largest wine production in Germany — hence the Weinstrasse!

What is a Diatomaceous Filter?

A prehistoric single celled algae provides an ideal filtering agent to bring wines and beers to the consuming brilliance preferred by Americans. The fluids are passed through this coarse, dust-like filter emerging clear of particles, satisfying to the eye and the taste buds!

What is a Digestif?

The French have a word for everything, including liqueurs. Digestifs for hundreds of years have been used after full meals as stomach restoratives. The fine bitters and cordials made of barks, quinine and seeds have done the job. *Vive le digestif!*

What is Distilling?

The alchemist may have failed in his search of gold, but he perfected the art of distillation. Heat is applied to wine or beer and the ethyl alcohol vaporizes to be cooled as a hard liquor. Vive le Difference!

d,e

What is Triple Distilling?

Once called the "whiskey of gentle authority" the spirits distilled on Erin Isle are indeed unique. But, it isn't the lilt of Irish laughter but the triple distilling which renders the end product so light and airy. The three-fold distillation assures a lightness and purity excellent for sipping and superb with coffee!

What is Doux?

The least popular of the French Champagnes goes by the name Doux — meaning sweet in French. The majority of Champagnes contain some concentration of the sweet, natural grape sugar called a 'dosage' added just before final corking. In Doux, the sugar level is at a very high ten percent.

What is Drip Irrigation?

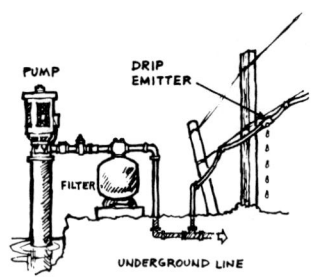

Fifty years ago, grape growers often flooded vinyards weekly with the mistaken notion that more fruit would develop. Over the years viticulturists have noted that grape vines produce best under stress. The latest technique of drip irrigation delivers the water drop by drop, akin to Chinese torture!

What is Enology?

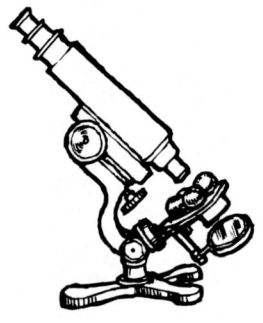

Enology (oenology) is the science of wine making. It is the chemistry of vinification — man's control of the whims of nature. The enologist harmonizes science with art to produce flawless vintages. He is the little old winemaker!

What is En Tirage?

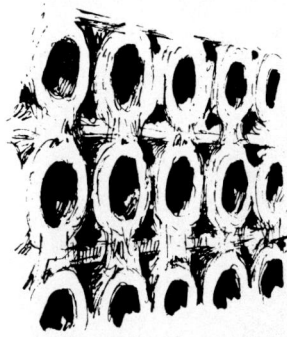

The charm and unique taste characteristics of French Champagne derive from the slow, secondary fermentation *en tirage*—in the bottle. From two to four full years, the wine intermingles with the yeast cells liberating nutrients and essences which create the tastes. Look for the delicate yeasty finish.

What is Entre-Deux-Mers?

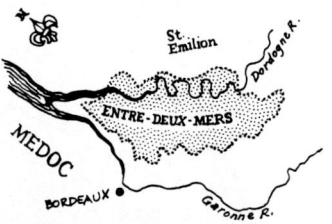

The translation *between two seas* literally refers to two rivers but more appropriately would apply to the sea of Bordeaux wines around Entre-Deux-Mers. Mostly white wines are produced in this 3200 acre section of little distinction. But what neighbors—St. Emilion, Pomerol and Medoc!

What are Grape Enzymes?

A very special place in winemaking history is reserved for Louis Pasteur for his discovery of the action of enzymes in grape must. These miniscule protein molecules trigger the complex chemical processes as grape sugars become ethyl alcohol and carbon dioxide. As many as twelve enzymes set in motion dozens of changes similar to the original creation of sugar in the vine. A symphony of nature!

What is EST! EST! EST!

Perhaps the most romantic of all wine tales was created by a servant who found a semi-sweet Montefiascone wine from Central Italy indescribably beautiful. His employer Bishop sent him ahead with instructions to write on the walls of taverns the condition of the wine served. Overwhelmed, he wrote: IT IS! IT IS! IT IS!

What are Esters?

While man is limited to four tastes he can readily distinguish hundreds of aromas. The esters in wines provide a profusion of distinct odors ranging from lilacs to green apples. These esters are compounds formed of acids and alcohols and they often change in aging and in the glass during consumption.

What is an Estufa?

The estufa or heated warehouse on the isle of Madeira is man's imitation of the hold of a sailing vessel. In Colonial times, the wine of Madeira was treasured for its smooth, aromatic finish which resulted from months at sea in tropic waters. The estufa is simply a heated warehouse in which the young wine cooks and ages!

What is Falernum?

Now that rum is again returning to the American scene, you may find a recipe which calls for a touch of Falernum. Unrelated to the Ancient Roman wine called Falerno, it is quite simply a syrup from the West Indies. Invented several hundred years ago, it is made by adding six percent alcohol to molasses syrup, lime, almonds, ginger and other spices. The perfect rum companion.

What is Fermentation?

Through all centuries men were mystified at the function of winemaking. Louis Pasteur found the answer in the middle of the last century to be small, airborne plant lives now called yeasts. These *ferments* break down the molecules of fruit or grain sugars creating ethyl alcohol and carbon dioxide. Voila—wine or beer!

What is Malolactic Fermentation?

A perfectly natural secondary fermentation occurs in wines, either in the cask or often in the bottle. A common bacteria, changes malic acid to lactic acid creating extra carbon dioxide bubbles. It is particularly desireable in some wines like the popular Lambrusco.

What is Charcoal Filtering?

Charcoal filters have the enviable capacity to remove undesirable elements from fluids. While used generously in whiskey-making, this technique is employed sparingly by winemakers particularly to remove color pigmentation when white wines have rested too long on their skins. Unfortunately, wine character is also lost!

What is Fish House Punch?

This popular colonial punch recipe was created in a famous social club of the same name formed in 1732 in Schuykill, Pennsylvania. Ideally blended hours or even days before consumption, the recipe calls for generous portions of rum, brandy, peach liqueur, loaf sugar, citrus juice, water and ice for cold service. No wonder its lasting popularity!

What Was a Colonial Flip?

Devotees of the modern flip appreciate their liquor smoothed with egg; sweetened with sugar; and topped with nutmeg. These are far from the original Colonial Flips which used strong beer, molasses, dried pumpkin and a shot of rum—all stirred up with a hot poker!

f

What is Flor?

The delicate, nut-like flavors of Spanish dry sherries derive from a unique, filmy yeast called flor. As if by magic, it forms in December in certain of the aging barrels. From these select barrels come the great fino and amontillado sherry wines.

What is Fraise?

Fraise or Creme de Fraise is a sweet, rich cordial with the flavor and aroma of fresh, ripe strawberries. Light red in hue, it is produced both from wild and cultivated fruit. The berries are macerated or soaked in alcohol to capture the delicate flavors and then distilled. Try Fraise with fruits and light cookies for dessert. You will love it.

What is Frascati?

The Italians call it *il sole nel bicchiere*—the sun in a glass. Such is the esteem for the most popular table wine in and around Rome. Produced primarily from two abundant local grapes—Malvasia and Trebbiano—Frascati is a white wine made both dry and semi-sweet. Try this bottled sunshine soon!

What is Frizzante?

Ask an Italian the meaning of frizzante and he will likely answer Lambrusco! The French call it pettilance and we term it sparkle. All refer to the slight carbonation in a beverage that delights the tongue. Lambrusco wine preeminently embodies this brush of effervescense.

What is Fusel Oil?

Fusel oils are congeners composed of higher alcohols present in most spirits—wines, liqueurs and liquors. In trace quantities, propyl, butyl, hexyl and heptyl alcohols provide the sharp, volatile tastes. Fusel oils provide the distinctive bite in bourbon or cognac, the taste you remember.

What is Gewurz-traminer?

f,g

Gewurz means spicy in German. Gewurztraminer is a delightful variety of the popular German and Alsatian traminer white grape. As its name implies, it nearly always yields a spicy, flowery bouquet and an intriguing, soft finish on the tongue. It is increasingly popular also in California. Try it as an aperitif.

What is Gin?

Good old Dutch professor Sylvius distilled grain spirits over fresh juniper berries for medicinal purposes. In the 17th Century, British soldiers shortened the word to gin and spread its effect throughout the empire. In addition to the tart juniper, other herbs used include cassia bark, fennel, almond, licorice and orange peel.

What are Gin Botanicals?

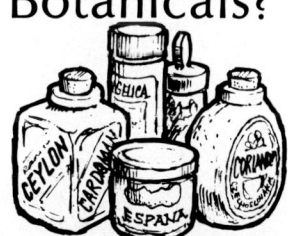

The most universal of all spirits in terms of ingredients must be gin! Originally named for the predominant botanical—the juniper berry—gin often contains essences of as many as a dozen spices. Angelica from Europe; coriander from Czechoslovakia; orange peel from Spain; cardoman from Ceylon. These and many others are introduced in a second distillation making gin the universal drink!

g

What is Hollands Gin?

The popular London Dry Gin is produced by redistilling neutral grain spirits over Juniper berry essences. The Dutch produce Hollands gin, sometimes called Genever, by using malty grain spirits. It's a heavy aromatic sipping drink, like cognac!

What is Old Tom Gin?

Old Tom was an enterprising British agent who made a sideline living dispensing gin through a funnel in his front door — probably the first recorded automat. In his name, Old Tom Gin is known throughout the world as a slightly sweet, English Gin. There is nothing dry about Old Tom!

What is Sloe Gin?

Neither slow, nor truly gin, this luscious brandy based, sweet, red cordial is made from sloe berries. The tiny purple plum berries grow on blackthorn bushes. The cordial has a flowery melon aroma and a tart almondy taste. Try a sloe gin fizz for frothy delight.

What is a Governo?

The gastronomically inventive Italians long ago perfected a system for producing zesty, high alcohol, high tannin wines to complement rich pastas. Called the governo in Chianti wine making, it involved a second fermentation in December from grapes dried on huge trays. For the paisano, it is *vin ordinaire, extra-ordinaire!*

What is Grape Bloom?

Over the centuries, the grape berry has developed the perfect covering to protect its precious fruit and to assist the willing winemaker. Called a waxy bloom, the sticky substance on ripe grapes acts as a suntan lotion protecting the fruit. Of greater importance, the air borne fermentation yeasts stick and adhere to the wax. A wonder of nature!

What is Grape Must?

g

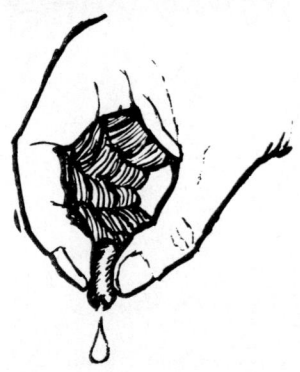

Fresh grape juice is called must by the winemaker. The pulp and the juice alone are colorless and therefore make white wine. For red or rose wines, the winemaker leaves the skins and seeds in the fermenting tank.

What are Grape Sugars?

Very early in the life of man, wine became a staple food. This ancient accident came about because of the predominance of glucose and fructose in the juice of the grape. Unlike many other sugars produced in nature, these two are instantly fermentable in the presence of yeast. Other more complex sugars are present in trace amounts even in the driest of vintages. But, it is glucose and fructose that make the grape berry so very special!

What is Grappa?

Leave it to the little old winemaker to make use of leftovers! A little water and a little yeast added to the pomace or squeezed grape skins will make a strong wine. That wine distilled into brandy is called Grappa in France or California or Eau de Vie De Marc in France. Wherever, it is fiery, white lightning!

g,h

What is a Graves Wine?

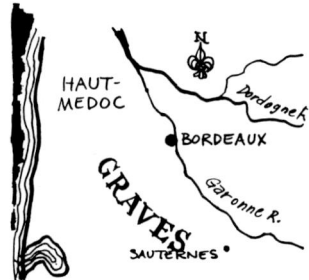

Novices often associate the Bordeaux area of France exclusively with rich, red Cabernet wines. The forty mile long, twelve mile wide district encompassing Bordeaux city actually produces more whites than reds. Meaning gravel in French, Graves whites are dry, crisp and the match of white Burgundy.

What is Grenadine?

Since it is often found in cocktail recipes, many consider Grenadine an alcoholic liqueur. To the contrary, it is simply a smoothly sweet syrup concocted from pomegranites, strawberries, raspberries and similar fruits. It blends best with whiskey.

What is Grog?

Grogram was a popular heavy cloth in the 1700's made from silk and wool. One popular British Admiral named Edward Vernon wore a distinctive grogram coat. Vernon began to dilute with water, the daily ration of rum he gave his sailors. They affectionately named the new drinks Old Grog!

What is a Hangover?

The French call it wood of the mouth; the Germans call it Katzenjammer or wailing of the cats; in Italy it is Stonato or out of turn. Wherever experienced, overindulgence in beverage alcohol of any form produces both physical and psychological fatigue, headache, and often nausea. Doctors feel a combination of dancing and stress produce the fatigue while toxic congeners irritate cranial arteries. It all can be avoided by moderation!

Who was Agoston Harazthy?

Every wine-lover in America should possess a portrait of this far-sighted and industrious Hungarian nobleman. In 1861, he convinced Gov. Downey of California to send him to Europe to procure grapevines. His return with 100,000 cuttings of over 1400 varieties established California's thriving viticulture!

What are Heads and Tails?

Unlike the moonshiner, the modern whiskey distiller does not allow chance to determine his heads and tails. The heads and tails — foreshots and feints — are the most critical elements in his products — the tastes. These traces of esters, oils, acids and exotic higher alcohols are retained in controlled portions for flavor and bouquet.

What is Hermitage?

Rising majestically, pyramid-like, over the ancient French town called Tain lies a hill called Hermitage. The hill derives its name from a hermit who settled there following a Holy Land Crusade. Hermitage wines, mostly red from the noble Syrah grape, are among the heartiest in the world. Look for heavy tannin and fruity finish.

What is a Hogshead?

To mix a metaphor, the hogshead was the workhorse of the middle ages. In all its many forms and sizes, these barrels replaced the amphora as the common vessel for shipping fluids — wine, brandy, beer or oil. In Bordeaux it was called a Barrique, in Burgundy a Piece, in Spain a Butt.

h

What is a Hop Flower?

The pleasing, bitter taste in beer derives from the ripened cones of the flower of the female hop vine. First used at the Monastery of St. Denis in France in 760, hops are used worldwide but in lesser degree in modern light beers.

What is hops effect?

Near the end of the Middle Ages an extract called Humulus Lupulus was introduced into the brewing process. Hops at that time were thought to be a veritable pharmacopia, a cure-all. It turned out that hops provided not only tart flavor but also an anti-bacterial and a preservative to the brew.

What is Hospices de Beaune?

The charm and grace of the Burgundy area in France is magnificently exemplified in the Hospices or Hospital in the city of Beaune. Built in 1443, the hospital serves the poor of the area benefiting from the sale of wine from its own vineyards. Its famous auction on the third Sunday in November draws wine merchants from all over the world. Look for an Hospices Burgundy soon!

What is Liquor Hydrometer?

A common sight is the service station man testing anti-freeze with a glass hydrometer. The same gauged instrument measures specific gravity for both sugar content and alcohol content in liquor making. It is a gift from Ancient Greece in common use today!

What is Jerez Wine?

The Center of Spanish horse racing and bull fighting, the most romantic of all lands, is also the heart of the world of sherry wines. Jerez de la Frontera lies northeast of Gibraltar. Since the middle ages the Palomino grape has been fortified and aged in sun drenched soleras to become incomparable dry Amontillado or luscious sweet Oloroso. Jerez is Sherry!

What is the Juniper Berry? j,k

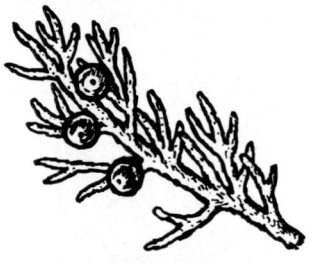

One of the commonest of evergreen shrubs throughout the world is the juniper. There are thirteen species in the United States alone. The berry which grows on the female plant secretes an oil similar to the hop cone used in beer. The juniper berry oil is the dominant flavoring in gin along with many other herbs such as anise, licorice, coriander and caraway. In fact the word gin is a corruption of the Dutch word for juniper — GENEVER!

What is a Kiddush Cup?

The Kiddush is a blessing recited over wine on the Jewish Sabbath and on holidays. The head of the household chants the prayers in thanksgiving for creation and delivery from bondage. Everyone then partakes of the wine which is usually quite sweet though it may be any type certified by a Rabbi.

What is Kirschwasser?

Kirsch or kirschwasser is a high proof, colorless and completely dry brandy distilled from the small black cherry indigenous to central Europe. Do not mistake it for the popular very sweet Creme de Kirsch. The cherry is nearly as universal as the grape in its food and liquor uses!

k, l

What is Kummel?

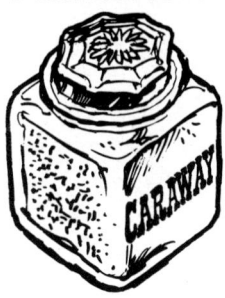

A most popular liqueur throughout Northern Europe, KUMMEL [pronounced KIM - EL] is distilled from grain and flavored with caraway and often a dash of cummin. It is pure white, dry to medium sweet and usually sold at 80 proof. Try it after dinner, or as accent to your cocktails.

What is Kvass?

Now that Americans are allowed as tourists in Russia, a new and different beer taste is being acquired. Common both as commercial and home brew, Russian Kvass beer is flavored with mint and cranberries!

What is a Proprietary Label?

In the liquor business, a proprietary label is one created by the wine maker or distiller. The ingredients in the bottle may be common knowledge, as in wines, or they may be jealously guarded secret recipes as in Benedictine. No other company may use the name.

What is Labrusca?

The Vikings found a profusion of grape-bearing vines in North America. All were of a common family that readily withstand the coldest of winters called *Vitis labrusca* grapes. Ideal for juice, jam, jelly and luscious as fresh fruit, Labruscas make poor wines. Common types are Concord, Catawba, Niagara and Delaware.

What is Lacrima Christi?

One of the most romantic of all wine tales surrounds the dry, white golden wines produced from the crumbling lava of Mt. Vesuvius in Tuscany. According to tradition, Lucifer fell from heaven into the Bay of Naples. The good Lord grieved to see the sinful fellow and shed an immortal tear—Lacrima Christi—from which the vineyards grew!

What is Cold Lagering?

Long ago, in the Middle Ages, German monks discovered the unique alchemy when a fresh young brew was stored for a short period in cool caves. In this quiet, cool period, the beer clears as suspended solids coagulate and descend to the bottom of the tanks. The bright and crystal clear brew you love comes from patient weeks in very cool cellars.

What is Lambrusco?

The Veneto area of North Central Italy has yielded two inestimable gifts to the world—the sausage and Lambrusco wine! From the grape of the same name, Lambrusco is a zesty, fruity, slightly carbonated and nearly always medium sweet red wine. A beautiful beginning red!

What is L'Chayim?

The Jewish toast to health familiar round the world is L'Chayim. It is given, of course, with wine. The toast celebrates Hebrew Yaykin, the wine which Noah made and consumed after the Flood. L'Chayim — TO YOUR HEALTH!

What is Le Part Des Anges?

The brandy called cognac is aged for years in warehouses called Chais above ground unlike wine caves. About three percent of the precious fluid evaporates from the barrels filling the air in Cognac town with the equivalent of 12 million bottles of brandy per year. The French say it is The Angels Share!

What was the Liberty Tree?

In colonial days, the tavern was the community center, the post-office, the government rooms as well as the social hall. Helping to plot the Revolution, a band of wealthy men met as a secret society called The Sons of Liberty. For protection, they gathered in a tree house in what they called The Liberty Tree outside of Montagne's Tavern in New York City.

What is Liebfraumilch?

There is little doubt of the popularity of this light, slightly sweet blended wine from the Rhine river in Gemany. It is truly the popular taste. Tradition has the name emanating from the famous church in Mainz called Liebfrauenkirch. More probably it is simply Lieblich which means light, pleasant wine!

What is Limestone Water?

As Scotch and Irish immigrant farmers moved westward to the hills of Kentucky, they discovered more than fertile soil. The fresh cold waters flowing from rocky springs were nearly mineral free. The limestone shelf extending to Tennessee, Illinois and through Kentucky purifies the water — and iron free water makes good whiskey! Little wonder Bourbon caught on!

What is a Liqueur?

Originally medicinal remedies and nostrums, cordials or liqueurs are mixtures of liquor — usually brandy — with pleasant flavors including fruits, peels, pits, seeds, leaves and spices. Always sweet, sometimes very sweet, nice for desserts.

What is Liquer d'Or?

A delight among the profusion of French Herbal Liqueurs is d'or. The word refers to the quite visible flecks of pure gold suspended in the fluid. Made from lemon peels, herbs and plants, d'or is reminiscent of yellow Chartreuse with a mysterious, lingering finish on the palate.

What is Liquor Tax?

Man's pleasures and follies are prime targets of the tax collector. The first excise tax on whiskey was imposed in 1791 to help defray the enormous debts of the Revolution. That first tax of less than a cent a gallon rose to $6.40 during World War I and to the present $10.50. It is a major source of federal dollars.

What is a Liter?

To lovers of imported wines, the metric system of measurement is well known. In January 1979, all shipments of American wine conformed to these international standards. The liter or about 33.8 ounces is the standard. Three quaters of a liter or 750 milliliters will replace the familiar fifth. The tenth or half bottle of wine will contain 375 milliliters. Very little difference occurs in these smaller sized but the gallon will be replaced by 3 liters or only 101 fluid ounces. Oh well, we'll get use used to it!

l,m

What is the Loire Valley?

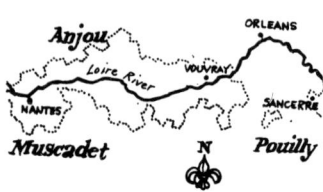

Running west through the heart of France, the Loire river and its valley provides breathtaking scenery, medieval castles and stunning vineyards. From the dry Pouilly at Sancerre, through the light Vouvray and Anjou Rose' to the salty dry Muscadet, the wines are distinctive and enchanting.

What is Maceration?

Liqueur maceration is the age-old technique of infusing rich fruit aromas and tastes into after-dinner cordials. High proof spirits, usually brandies, are placed in a tank with the crushed fruit pulp. The mixture is steeped, like tea, for days or months creating a glorious wedding of interests!

What is Madeira?

On a forbidding, volcanic isle 500 miles southeast of Portugal, rugged farmers reap their harvest and carry the grape juice in twelve gallon goat skins to the winemakers. The wines are then stored in heated warehouses for six months producing the longest lived and best of all dessert wines. Madeira! Marvelous Madeira!

What is Maderized Wine?

Wines—particularly white wines—that show a browning effect are said to be maderized. The causes are often poor storage, exposure to air or simply keeping a delicate white overlong. The true Madeira wine taste by contrast is a desirable baked tang.

What is Malt Liquor?

All brew is composed of malt, hops and water. But malt liquor has the considerable advantage of up to 6.5% alcohol by weight as contrasted to the 4% or less alcohol in regular beers. In addition, hotter fermentations yield lighter body and often sweeter tastes.

What is Malted Grain?

Malting is one of the stages in the life cycle of grain which is caused by the application of heat and moisture. The grains produce new shoots by germinating. The grain starches are transformed into maltose, a sugar, which can be yeast fermented producing beer. Malting is a must to produce beer and hard liquor.

What is Mandarine?

Most of the familiar citrus fruit liqueurs are made from sweet and bitter orange peels. A popular exception is Mandarine developed from sweet tangerines. Bright orange in color, overwhelmingly sweet, it is best used as a cocktail or punch flavoring.

What is Marc?

The oldest and most universal of all spirit brandies is *eau-de-vie-de-marc*. Marc is the pomace or pulp left after wine has been fermented and racked. In the Burgundy area, it traditionally was packed under clay until mid-winter; watered; and refermented before distilling. Many well known vineyards produce this marc including Romanee-Conti, Musigny and Chamberlin.

m

What is Maraschino?

Tart maraschino cherries from Dalmatia, Yugoslavia are used to make this bitter-sweet delight. The cherry stones are distilled separately to be combined with the pomace of the fruit. Aged in neutral hickory wood, Maraschino is sold often in wicker bottles.

What is Marsala?

The famed and beloved dessert wine of Italy is incomparable Marsala. Though at times found in dry versions, most Marsala is sweet and walnut brown in color with a slight acid undertone. Marsala Speciales are blended with popular tastes such as banana, mocha and strawberry for perfect desserts.

What is Mash?

There is no record of when man first discovered the magical effects of steeping grain in hot water. Chemically, the enzyme diastase converts the grain starches to fermentable sugars. The fermented mash becomes beer and the distilled beer becomes whiskey. It all begins with the mash.

What is Mastikha?

Leave it to the Greeks and their love of resins to produce a liqueur from the Mastic tree which grows on the Island of Chios. Like their popular resined wines, Mastikha is quite dry with a tangy, woody finish.

What is Mavrodaphne?

In 1845 a Bavarian named Gustav Clauss settled in Patros, Greece and founded a winery now world famous — Achaia-Clauss. He produced a rich, muscat-tinged sweet dessert wine called Mavrodaphne. Of immense popularity yet today, myth has it he named it for the love of his life who reminded him of the enchanted goddess, Daphne.

What is Mead?

Mead was the favorite drink of the Anglo-Saxon. This soft concoction may even have preceded grape wine and is in a class by itself being neither fruit nor grain in origin. Honey and water are allowed to ferment, often with flavoring herbs to produce luscious mead.

What is the Medoc?

Without question and without parallel, the Medoc extending fifty miles north and west of Bordeaux is the best red wine area of the world. Smaller in size than the Napa Valley, the area produces principally the great cabernet sauvignon vintages with such famous names as Margaux, St. Julian, Listrac, Moulis, Saint Estephe and Pauillac. Magnificent!

What is Mercurey?

To the confirmed wine lover, Mercurey is neither planet nor messenger of the gods but a superbly soft French red wine. Produced from the same Pinot Noir grapes as the famous Beaune vineyards to the North, Mercurey has earned a world-wide acceptance. One bottle will convince you!

m

What is Mezcal?

If Tequila is the gentle spirit of the Mexican nobleman, Mezcal is the drink of the peon. Like Tequila, it is produced from a variation of cactus called the Dumpling. Following a short fermentation of the juice and heart, there is a single distillation. The spirit sold at 100 proof is said to contain traces of the hallucinogen mescaline!

What is a Microclimate?

Through untold seasons of history, wine grape growers have recorded the absolutely ideal pockets of geography which mature the very best wine grapes. Today, the scientists intensively study the wind, the sun, the soil, the fog, the frost and any other elements that will affect grape maturity. The really great wines emerge from these minute microclimates.

What is The Midi?

The vast stretch of land from the Rhone river in southern France to Spain comprises the Midi. From a sheer production viewpoint, it produces an astounding five percent of the world's wines and nearly a third of France's heavy consumption. Like the arid hot San Joaquin valley of California, it produces everyday wines in profusion!

What is Moonshine?

Moonshine is the raw, unaged liquor often called "mountain dew" which is produced on illegal stills often of very low quality. As early as the 18th century, illegal brandy or gin smuggled into England and Ireland was termed moonshine. Five thousand illegal stills were seized in 1973 alone and billions in taxes have been lost due to these clandestine enterprises. To be certain, buy legitimate!

What is Moselle Wine?

The easiest way to distinguish a Moselle wine is by the dark green bottle. Rhine wines are in similar brown bottles. A better way is to enjoy the charming, light, fragrant and often dry Reisling vintages. A combination of slate soil and crisp, cool climate produces the very best German wines. The prevailing cool climate prompts grape growers to cut back the leaves to catch every ray of sunshine on the terraced sloping vineyards. You'll love the Moselle!

What is Moulin au Vent?

The King of the popular Beaujolais vintages is undoubtedly Moulin Au Vent. The name derives from a stone windmill set amidst the vast fields of grapes. It is a noble, big, Gamay wine and one of the few from the region that ages well.

What is a Mull?

Before central heating, warding off winter's chill took on many forms. The mull was a favorite warmer. Basically, mulls are sugared and spiced hot drinks made from a base of wine, beer or cider. For effect, brandy, rum and aquavit were added either singly or together. Little wonder our forefathers had a tendency to "mull over" thorny questions!

What is Muy Anejo?

Most everyone recognizes popular Tequila as a light, colorless nearly neutral spirit that mixes easily in any drink. Small amounts of Tequila are aged in used whiskey barrels acquiring a soft, golden hue. Two or more years in wood is Muy Anejo!

n,o

What is a Negociant Eleveur?

Winemaking is the largest commercial enterprise in France. Over hundreds of years a wine middleman has emerged called a Negociant — literally a shipper-merchant. He buys wines, blends wines and ships finished wines gaining important credibility to his labels. Of even greater importance is his role as technician, adviser and Indian Chief to the thousands of independent growers.

What is a Neutral Spirit?

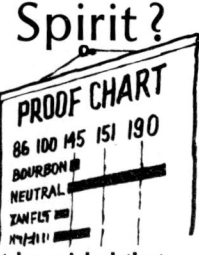

Do not be misled that neutral spirits are any less potent than those familiar liquors containing the smells and tastes of the grains or fruits. A neutral spirit by law is ethyl alcohol taken from the still at 190 proof or above--that is 95 percent pure ethanol without a discernable trace of the grain or other distilling material. Vodka is normally a neutral spirit diluted with distilled water.

What is Noble Rot?

Noble Rot or botrytis cinerea is a curious variation of the air-born molds that attack ripe grapes. Filaments of the mold penetrate the grape skins without damaging the fruit. The juice is depleted thereby concentrating the grape sugars which will produce luscious, creamy wines.

What is Oak Char?

The inside of a bourbon whiskey barrel of new oak has been blackened over raging gas fires. The resulting layers of dark char, soft carmel and pure oak combine as catalysts for chemical aging and produce both tart flavor and ruddy hue. They allow air in for oxidizing and water out.

O

What is Limousin Oak?

An extraordinary marriage of nature is the Quercus Robur — hard oaks — of the Limousin forests and the distillation called Cognac from nearby provinces. In the late middle ages, this oak was chosen to hold the young brandy. Soon was observed an unusual mellowing effect on long stored spirits. Some cognac is now aged up to twenty years! Limousin oaks imparts special character to spirits or wines unmatched by other woods throughout the world.

What is Ocha?

An unusual and pleasing liqueur comes to us from Japan. Also sometimes called Suntory Green Tea Liqueur, Ocha is produced by steeping bitter, rolled tea leaves in brandy and neutral spirits. Retaining the tea bitterness, Ocha contains up to fifty percent sugar for a very sweet finish.

What is Oke?

Sojourners to our Fiftieth state soon become acquainted with Okolehao, a favorite local spirit taken on the rocks or in highball form. Distilled from a mash compounded of the sacred Ti plant, molasses and rice, Oke is sold in Crystal Clear and Golden hues at 80 proof. It is the liquid Lei!

What is the Olfactory Sense?

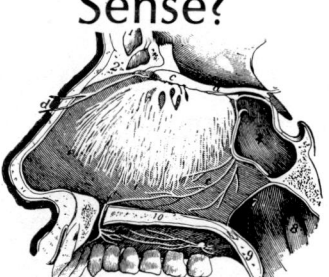

While man is limited to four tastes, he can distinguish up to ten thousand odors. Molecules are volatized as vapors and they are carried up the nasal passages to the olfactory nerves. The brain reacts favorably or is repulsed. Hence the sense of smell is integral to the enjoyment of beverage alcohols.

p

What is Ouzo?

Ouzo is the pungent, anise flavored liqueur of the Greek. Reminiscent of French Pernod, it is sold at ninety proof and is brandy based. It is best served with very cold water — about four ounces of water to one of Ouzo. It blends milky white and is a refreshing aperitif or dessert.

What is the Palate?

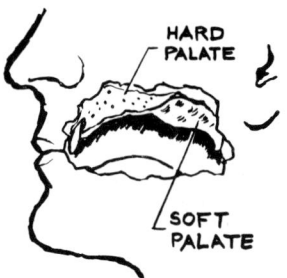

Wine lovers should be particularly thankful for the palate — the bony-muscular separation between mouth and nasal cavity. The hard palate forms the roof of the mouth and the soft creates the throat closure. Both contain sensitive taste buds. Great wines are always *palatable!*

What is Passerilage?

In the torrid Languedoc area of Southern France, there is produced a profusion of rich dessert wines. The objective of high alcohol and high sugar is achieved in a unique grape growing technique. The canes are tied below the fruit to cut the flow of sap from the fruit. The sugar concentrates for the rich, mellow wines!

What is Pastis?

Pastis is the happy successor to universally banned Absinthe. Concocted from neutral spirits and herb flavorings, the dominant flavor is from aniseed. A favorite of French fishermen, it is usually diluted with water or served over the ice. A superb thirstquencher!

What is Peat Reek?

When something is overpowering in odor, it is common to say it 'reeks'. This is literally true for Scotch whiskey revered world-wide for its smoky flavor. The ground barley malt is dried over heaps of burning peat acquiring the acrid, oily flavor unique to Scotch.

What is Persian Poison?

Shah Djemsheed in Persia always kept a bowl of grapes by his bedside. According to ancient lore, one day he found some of his fruit fermented and he marked it poison. A neglected harem girl drank it planning suicide. The gentle intoxication delighted her and she brought her discovery to the Shah. Both lived happily thereafter!

What is Persico?

Persico is an oh-so-light cordial which dates back to 18th Century England made from fresh peaches. The delicate peach flavor is lighter and more difficult to capture in liquors than many other fruits. Therefore the peach is more often used as an accent to other juices in cordials as in the popular Southern Comfort.

What are Petite Chateaux?

For the serious student of wines as well as the casual buyer, the Bordeaux Petite Chateau can represent the glorious lucky find or a mediocre to unsatisfying bottle. In times of short supply, many of the three thousand or so small vineyards seek market acceptance under their own, unclassified labels. Seek advice from your wine merchant and enjoy the hunt!

p

What is Phylloxera?

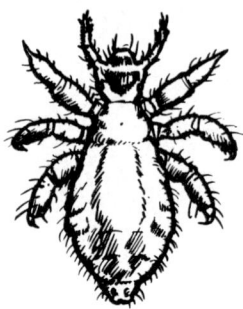

Phylloxera vastatrix is a native American plant louse of the familiar aphid family. This pesky critter burrows into the tender roots of grapevines literally sapping their energies. It nearly devastated the world's vineyards last century. Now almost all grape types are grafted on hardy, resistant American grape rootstock.

What is Pilsner?

Pilsner originated in the Bohemian town of Pilsen in 1292. A particular strain of hops from that area yields a tart, pleasant aroma and taste, and the local yeast produces a light brew. Other light brews around the world have borrowed the name but never matched the original!

What is a Pina?

The heart of the Blue Agave plant grown extensively in Mexico and South America is termed a *pina* — or pineapple which it closely resembles. It takes up to ten years to mature the plant pina which under steaming and pressure will yield up to 30 pounds of molasses. Fermented and distilled this pina juice is called *tequila*.

What is Pineau Des Charentes?

A worker's accident some four hundred years ago led to the most popular aperitif-liqueur in Southern France. Pineau des Charentes is produced only in the Cognac region and is made by blending new cognac brandy into fresh grape juice. Then aged like fine brandy, Pineau is clean and fruity as an aperitif over ice! It is the only aperitif under the Appellation Controlee.

What is Poire William?

The most distinctive of all fruit brandy is that distilled from ripe Williams and Bartlett pears. Though very difficult to ferment and distill, the resulting spirit has intense fruit aroma and delicate taste. A beautiful aperitif!

What is Piquette?

Through untold centuries, the wine ration for French vineyard workers has been the Piquette. It is made from a fermentation of water and the discarded skins and pips of the regular vintage. Low in alocohol and high in acid it is a satisfactory bonus and infinitely better than the water!

What is Pisco?

Pisco is grape brandy, distilled from mellow muscat grapes near the port town of Pisco in Southern Peru. Appreciated world-wide, its fame grew from celebrated Pisco Punch in gold rush days of San Francisco. It is unaged, pure white and fiery. Try it in a sour!

What is Pommard?

In the very heart of the Cote de Beaune, lies one of the greatest of the French Burgundy wine districts — Pommard. The 850 acres of prime land produce a scant one hundred thousand or so cases of deep red, full bodied Pinot Noir wines. The better Pommard also identify the specific vineyard as in Epenot or Les Cambes. Pommard and quality — *tout la meme!*

What is Tawny Port?

Now that ports and sherries are recognized as after dinner delights, the world has discovered the finesse and charm of the noble Tawny Port. Softer, less fruity than Ruby Port, this rich port gains its tawny color from long years of aging in wood. Try it with cheese instead of dessert!

What is Wooded Port?

The great Port wine from Portugal is aged in wood in a system similar to the Spanish Solera system. Wine is blended barrel to barrel during aging. The style of each shipper is dominant as these wooded port blends contain as many as thirty different wines. Egg whites are used to clean the wine of sediment every year or so producing drier, tawny colored and luxuriously soft wines.

What is Vintage Port?

All Port wines are great but few are vintaged. As with French Champagne, only the very best years in Portugal are set aside for individual barrel aging of two to three years. Then these superb, mellow ports are bottled and rest for at least another ten years. Uniquely, both the vintage year and the bottling year show on the label.

What is Porter?

The English enjoy their beers sweet and warm. Porter, named for the waiters who deliver it, is a top-fermenting ale. It is dark brown from the roasted malt used in brewing and has a heavy, pleasing foam with just a touch of hops. Three cheers for the Porters!

What is Porto?

O Porto means The Port. Since ancient times this lovely Portugese town has been the center of commerce for the rich, red dessert wines produced in the upper Douro river. First as consumers and later as merchants, the British carried this wine throughout the civilized world.

What is Poteen?

To an Irishman, a poteen is a small pot. It is also illegal whiskey produced in small pot stills over untold centuries in hidden bogs of that romantic land. Descendants of these poteen makers settled in the hills of Kentucky and created American moonshine!

What is Pouilly Fuisse'?

The almost unpronounceable, newly popular white wine from France is named for two close hamlets — Pouilly and Fuisse'. Very dry like the Chablis to the north, it is produced from the elegant Chardonnay grape and is excellent for any light entree.

What is a Pousse-Cafe?

Showy Pousse-Cafe drinks are formed by floating layers of Liqueurs. Pour over an inverted teaspoon and they may be prepared and refrigerated in advance. Try a Patriotic — first red Creme de Noyaux; next white Creme de Menthe and then glistening blue Curacao. Salute!

What is Proof?

American proof is twice the actual alcohol content. 100 proof bourbon has 50% alcohol. 200 proof is pure alcohol. Wine, which shows 12% alcohol By Volume on the label is, therefore, 24 proof.

What is a Proof Gallon?

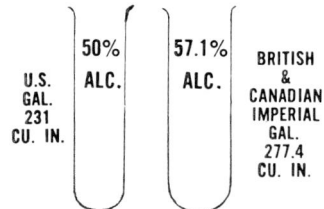

The inventor of the hydrometer left a legacy of confusion for the alcohol consumer. He named the alcohol as proof where the hydrometer floated—at the odd level of 57.1 percent of alcohol by volume. Fortunately or not, our federal officials changed the formula of proof to exactly half of the volume as alcohol—hence a proof gallon. Confused? So is everyone else but the tax collector!

What is Gunpowder Proof?

The confusing term *proof* originated innocently enough from the practice of early booze peddlers giving proof of alcohol in their blends. Equal parts of gunpowder and the liquor were lit with a match. At exactly fifty percent alcohol, a nice blue flame resulted. Hence proof today is twice the actual alcohol content.

What is the Highest Proof Liquor?

If you are looking for high, high proof, look to imported rums. Some is sold up to 194 proof, and that is ninety seven percent pure ethanol. The remaining three percent fluid is mostly water though it may have chemical traces of the molasses it was made from.

What is a Proprietary Cordial?

In the late sixteenth century, the cordial became a significant beverage. At this period most were mixtures of brandy and exotic herbs, flowers and spices desired for their delicate shades in taste. The secret recipes could not be easily copied so names such as Chartreuse or Benedictine survived as unique products—purchased only from the proprietary firm. Proprietary labels command a large and growing share of the market!

What is Provence?

Wine books and wine lovers rave over the glories of Burgundy and Bordeaux but seldom mention lowly Provence. The glorious sun baked coast of Southern France was planted to grapes by the Phoenecians. Caesar favored its wines. Alas, today the predominantly hot climate produces high alcohol, low acid vintages of little distinction. Provence is, however, the most heavily cultivated grape district in the world!

What is Grape Pruning?

The industrious Romans are credited with the early perfection of this art which seeks to select out a limited number of buds for the following year's fruit. It creates the balance between quantity and quality and is accomplished in mid-winter by skilled craftsmen who cut away the old wood. Great wines come from great pruners!

What is a Pub?

A Pub is a Public House. In England and pioneer America, the Public House was an integral unit of society. Serving often as post office, courtroom, inn, restaurant and barter house as well as social center. Many of the historic meetings leading to our revolution and freedom were held in Pubs!

p,r

What is Pulque?

Manana is manageable to the Mexican through the magic of pulque—his native beer. The productive Maguey cactus will yield up to twelve gallons a day of sweet sap which is fermented in leather to a six percent brew. The same brew distilled is known as Tequila!

What is Qualitatswein?

The range of types and classifications of German wines became so complex and mysterious that a single quality code was adopted in 1971. Eleven regions were designated as Quality or Qualitatswein. In addition each could be further qualified by a *Pradikat.* In ascending order these pradikat are Cabinett, Spaetlese, Auslese, **Beerenauslese and Trocken** enauslese. Still confused?

What is a Quinta?

Perhaps the most romantic and difficult terrain on the earth given to grape growing lies amid the upper Douro river cliffs in Portugal. Here the grapes for the reknowned ports are grown in **agricultural estates called quintas. Steep, forbidding and dramatically terraced estates dazzle the eye and challenge the grape picker!**

What is Ratafia?

Ratafia originally were the sweet drink concoctions made to drink at the signing of treaties. A whole series of apertifs came to be called Ratafia usually made with soft fruit like raspberries or strawberries. A few are still produced in France like Ratafia de Bourgogne and Ratafia de Champagne.

What is Recioto?

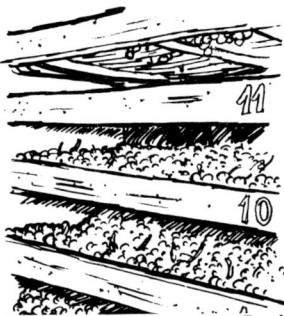

A unique process creates Recioto near the beautiful town of Verona in northern Italy. Called *passito*, specially picked very ripe grapes are placed in shallow, cane bottomed trays to dry until January. A slow fermentation of forty five days is followed by another of eighteen months. The result is, very high alcohol production. It is made in dry, sweet and sparkling versions.

What is Remuage?

Remuage is French for "shaking" and that is exactly what the French do to their bottle fermenting champagne. A trained *Remueur* turns up to 32 thousand bottles in a day, helping to settle the sediment in the neck of the bottle.

What is Retsina?

Since ancient times, the Greeks have flavored wines with pine resin. Nearly half of the white and rose' wines produced for local consumption are thusly treated. Try one as an aperitif or a conversation piece. But, recognize Retsina as an acquired taste!

What is the Rheingau?

The drama of the medieval castles along the Rhine is surpassed only by the annual joust with nature to pick the grape harvest as late as possible. The superb late harvested Rieslings sometimes as late as December occur in a stretch of the river from Hockheim to Bingen. Protected from the north winds, the grapes grow old and become concentrated in sugar. Over three thousand grape growers produce extraordinary vintages on a scant six thousand acres. Rheingau — Rhine Glory!

What is the Rheinpfalz?

The warmest and most productive agricultural area of Germany extends along the upper Rhine, to the French border, and is called the Rheinpfalz. Because the Haardt Mountains protect it from the cold north winds, the area produces many Spaetlese (late harvest) grapes. The wines of the region are soft in flavor, and are the standard carafe drink of Germany.

What is the Rioja?

The truly great table wines of Spain originate on the banks of the River Ebro. This northeastern section has a milder climate in both summer and winter conducive to the production of both dry and sweet wines. All three types—Tinto, Blanco and Rose abound. Look for the Riserva on the label for the best vintages.

What is Rock and Rye?

Old wives tales were based on practical observations. One of the most satisfying was a dose of Rock and Rye as a nostrum for the common cold. The rye was rye whiskey, the rock was a combination of lemons, oranges, cherries and other fresh fruits and rock candy syrup. Old wives noticed the pleasant results from this liqueur!

What is Rum?

The bloodthirsty pirate, the proper British soldier, and the American colonist shared a partiality for rum. Rum is made from cane sugar. Picked; crushed; boiled to molasses; fermented; and finally distilled into rum. Light rum is enjoying a new popularity in our nation.

What is Barbados Rum?

As early as 1775, our forefathers consumed prodigious amounts of West Indy Rum. The Barbados Island soil is composed of volcanic ash and yields a cane sugar molasses which transforms into a heavy, smoky rum. It is best sipped and savored as compared to the light Puerto Rican types!

What is Martinique Rum?

Because of its unique characteristics, rum made Martinique the richest of all the Caribbean isles. Very much like American and Jamaican rums, Martinique is bold, flavorful and possessed of delightful bouquet. Try it over the rocks or as a flambe!

What is Puerto Rican Rum?

The national trend to light and white in beverage alcohol has lifted rum to widespread popularity. The lightest and the whitest of rums are made from molasses all over the Island of Puerto Rico. The Silver or White label type is the lightest of all and it outsells its fellow Golden Rum three bottles to one. Puerto Rican — the mixable, fixable rum!

What are Rum Types?

Of all beverage spirits, rums retain the greatest identity with their source material — molasses! Light Puerto Rican rum is fermented in half a day and distilled to high proof. Deep, dark Jamaican rums are fermented up to a week and distilled to heavy pungency in pot stills. So, pick your rum carefully and expect diversity in aroma and taste. You won't be disappointed!

What is Rumfustian?

Many colorful words have come into our language from the common use of rum in our Colonial days. The word rum itself derived from rumbullion which meant a tumult. A Rumfustian was a powerful punch which included a quart of beer, bottle of white wine, pint of gin, dozen egg yolks, spices and pint of rum! Quite a tumult!

What is Sangria?

In Spain, the hot districts of Tarragona and the La Mancha near Madrid, produce undistinguished red wines which come to life in the warming, tart punch called Sangria. The addition of Andalusian oranges and lemons plus apricot and sugar does the trick. Try it yourself with an inexpensive red. Olé and Salud!

What is Schnapps?

The most popular distilled spirit in the Scandinavian countries and in Germany is called Schnapps. It is the continental vodka. Made from potatoes or grain, it is white and neutral to the taste. In Hanover, they drink their beer and schnapps at the same time, artfully spilling one into the other on the way!

What is Peppermint Schnapps?

What a delight and what a difference is Peppermint Schnapps. To anyone who has quaffed the dry, fiery Germanic Schnapps, the cordial glass of the peppermint flavored variety is a new and rewarding experience. Try this one with mints and nuts after a full meal.

What is Scotch?

The Scots claim to have first distilled a malted grain in 1505 called *Usquebaugh* — later shortened to whisky. The key to the smoky scotch taste is literally the smoke of peat bog logs which are used to dry the malt. Scotch is a blend of many whiskies and is generally aged up to ten years. A truly unique spirit.

What is a Scotch Blend?

The true afficionado of scotch whisky should appreciate the long term and infinitely subtle steps that create distinctive scotch blends. As many as forty different aging whiskys about four years old are tested in standard wine glasses by sight, smell and taste. The light Highland and Lowland spirits predominate with accent from the pungent Campbelltown and Islay malts. Further aging follows the artful blending.

What is Single Malt Scotch?

Once the pride of all Scotsmen, a single malt scotch is now a rarity around the world. Popular scotches are blends of up to fifty whiskeys and spirits. The base of these blends is always the fiery, and hundred percent barley malt whiskey — the single malt. A great sipper like cognac!

What is Sekt?

The word *Sekt* in German is a corruption of the old English *sack* which referred to dry Spanish wine. Through more time and corruption it means today any German sparkling wine. The Germans are particularly fond of the bubbly, consuming over 100 million bottles annually. Export sparkling wines are usually titled *Schaumwein* but at home it is *Sekt!*

What is Sherry Wine?

Since the middle ages, an incomparable sipping and cooking wine has been made in Andalusia, southern Spain. It results from a post-fermentation mold which grows in flowers called FLOR on the new wine. The resulting wine has a baked, nutty character — The Sherry taste!

What is Fino Sherry?

One of the most charming and mysterious of grape wine stories is found in the development of a special mold called flor on aging sherry wine. Casks which develop these "flowers" are marked and set aside in Spain for the lightest, palest and most delicate of the nut-like fino sherries.

What is Flor Sherry?

In Spain, Flor means flower. One the rarest and most enchanting of the thousands of airborne fermenting yeasts is also called Flor. Found only in Jerez, Spain and the Jura Mountains of France, the yeast settles selectively on some of the aging sherries creating a thick mold. These lucky casks become the matchless, dry and nutty tasting Fino sherries.

Is Spanish Sherry Vintaged?

The customer who believes vintaging means quality will be forever disappointed in Spanish Sherry. *All sherries are blends* which are freely intermingled from distinct growing areas. Further, the solera system mixes the new with the old wines. Sherry is the triumph of the blender!

What was A Sling?

The earliest known record of a Sling was in 1768 in Colonial America. Gin was then at the height of its popularity in the British Empire. The gin was mixed with sweetened water, not unlike the highball of today. The Singapore Sling survives today little changed as the first, formal cocktail.

What is Slivovitz?

A favorite delicate liquor in Yugoslavia and other Eastern European nations is the plum brandy called Slivovitz. It is unique among fruit brandies as it is aged in wood barrels up to twelve years. This aging creates a straw color and slightly woody taste.

What is a Solera?

The solera system is composed of layers of barrels which blend and age fine Spanish sherries. The youngest wines enter the top barrels and work down through the years to be drawn from the bottom for sale. All sherry is thus blended wine.

What is Southern Comfort?

Bourbon is the base for this popular, luscious, peach flavored liqueur which has satisfied thousands since the civil war. Made popular again in Gone With The Wind, it provides a clean finish on the palate with moderate sweetness. Perfect for a mixer!

What Was the First American Spirit?

The world's oldest distilled spirit—Rum—was also the first commercial American spirit. About 1650, molasses from the Barbados was distilled to New England rum. John Adams wrote, "Molasses was an essential ingredient in American independence."

What is a Split Bottle?

Much confusion exists about a "split" of wine. The split is one quarter of the full bottle. The middle size is termed a half. The new metric bottles use the terms small, medium and regular.

What is Asti Spumante?

In the Piedmont of Northern Italy, there is made a luscious sweet sparkling wine unmatched in the world. Spumante means sparkling in Italian. Asti is the town. Muscat is the grape. They combine to produce a bubbly delight to accompany any dessert.

What is a Continuous Still?

Invented by a thrifty Scot liquor trader in 1832, the continuous still is basically a series of pot stills one upon the other. It has the very considerable financial advantage of running all day long with new product and of taking the liquor at any proof desired. Steam strips the alcohol from the beer or wine as it passes through.

What Is A Pot Still?

Distilling in its most fundamental form is accomplished—as any moonshiner knows—by applying wood fire or steam heat to wine or beer held in a pot. A funnel-like head directs the rising ethyl alcohol fumes through a cooling condenser and then to a jug. The resulting fluid is a hard liquor or the distilled spirit of the wine or beer in the tank.

What is Stout?

Every tourist in England can attest to the pungent aroma and bittersweet taste of the country's popular stout brew. Slightly higher in alcohol than lager beer, stout gets its pleasing taste from extra hops and distinctive malt.

What is Sugar-Acid Ratio?

Nothing in the romance and ancient lore of winemaking matches the balance of sugar and acids. Winemakers demand and pay highest prices for those grapes picked on the optimum day when these two elements are in perfect harmony. Too much sun respires the precious acids which give the pleasing bite to the wine!

What is Simple Syrup?

Simple syrup is simply done, but it is the reason for the creamy consistency of bar made specialty drinks and professional liqueurs. Simply boil a cup of water for a few seconds to boil out impurities and then add a cup of sugar. Simmer two minutes and you have a simple syrup!

What is Tafelwein?

Deutscher Tafelwein (literally German table wine) is the light, inexpensive, everyday table wine of Germany like the vin ordinaire of France.
The region of origin is usually named and the type of grape that makes up at least 75% of the wine inside.

What is a Tail Box?

The Kentucky moonshiner and the French Cognac distiller share a common production advantage. Both use the pot still which allows periodic tasting of the brandy or bourbon as it drips from the condenser. The modern distiller must depend upon a hydrometer enclosed in a "tail box" beyond touch or taste and under federal control. What price progress!

What are Taste Buds?

Nothing is more important or more taken for granted than the mystery of taste. Over ten thousand minute taste buds line the tongue and palate. These nerve endings transmit signals translating into sweet, sour or acid, bitter and salt. Psychologists argue that taste and smell form one harmonious function. A salute to the buds!

What was a Teetotaler?

In the latter half of the nineteenth century, the fuss and fury over prohibition rose to an emotional crescendo. The Laingsburg, Michigan Temperance Society offered two options in the form of Pledges. The first promised moderate drinking. The preferred second pledge of total abstinance was recorded with a "T." These enlistees for TEETOTALERS!

What is Tequila?

A light bodied liquor from cultivated agave cactus plants from central Mexico. The artichoke-like heart is mashed and fermented before distilling. A great cocktailer — as in Margarita!

What is Tete de Cuveé?

Literally, the tete de cuveé is the top of the barrel. For many years, this phrase was used in France to describe the very best wines, and is still widely used by wine journalists. The phrase was officially replaced in 1935 by Grand Cru, a broader term that can relate both to the wines and the vineyards.

What is a Tip?

In our pioneer days, the town tavern was literally the town center providing food, lodging, drink, military rooms, courtrooms, postal services and so on. Patrons were urged to place offerings in a box on the wall which would be divided among the servants TO INSURE PROMPTNESS! If someone forgot, a servant would often whisper TIP!

What is Tokaji Azsu?

Tokaji Azsu is the delightful dessert wine of Hungary made from the Furmint grape. Its imitations in the west are called Tokay. The word Azsu means the late gathered grapes which have sweetened and concentrated with noble rot. These Azsu grapes are added to the fermenting wines in pails or puttonys to enrich the blends.

t, u

What is American Tokay?

Don't be puzzled by the similarity in names. American Tokay is a pleasant, medium-sweet blend of Sherry and Port with perhaps a touch of Angelica. Additionally, it is strengthened with brandy alcohol. While a fine after dinner toasting wine, it is far removed from the famous white, Hungarian Tokai.

What is Triple Sec?

Perhaps the most common of all cordials is Triple Sec. It is produced in many countries using the bittersweet oils in orange peels. Twist a peel over a flame and these oils will spark and burn. For sipping or as a cocktail ingredient, Triple Sec is smooth and satisfying!

What is Trockenbeer Enauslese?

Perhaps the most difficult to pronounce German wine is most certainly the most luscious of all. Very late harvesting of individual sun-ripened, shriveled berries — that's what the word means in German — creates high sugar, unbelievably mellow wines. Phonetically, its pronounced: TROKE - EN - BEER - EN - OUS - LAY - ZAH.

What is Uisge Beatha?

The first whiskey of man is thought to have originated in the rolling hills of Ireland. Irish legend even claims St. Patrick as the first whiskey maker. As early as the tenth century, mention is found in Gaelic of Uisge Boatha, or water of life. The Irish have a word for it!

What is Ullage?

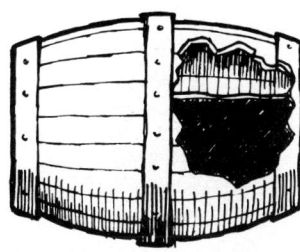

By definition, ullage is nothing—the empty space at the head of a barrel or bottle. By common usage ullage is the amount of wine or liquor that evaporates through the sides of the aging vessel. To prevent spoilage in barrels, winemakers fill this ullage once each month!

What is Valpolicella?

u,v

The long, narrow Valpolicella valley in Northeast Italy provides the matchless beauty of Lake Garda, and the setting for Romeo and Juliet. The star-crossed lovers undoubtedly drank the light, refreshing red wines of the area, now world famous. Produced from several varieties of Grapes, Valpolicella is the Italian Beaujolais — light, fruity, and fragrant — a wine to be enjoyed in its youth!

What is VDQS?

Be on the lookout for this designation on imported French wines. Often you will find both quality and price in your favor. In 1949, this designation was coined—Vin Delimité de Qualité Superieure—limited wines of good quality. A step below the famous Controlée vintages, these growths are still carefully controlled and are excellent wines.

What is a Venencia?

The mystery and lore of Sherry is matched only by the men who make it. One of these cellar artists uses a Venencia made of whalebone with a silver cup at the tip. It is used to test the clarity of the aging wine. Thrust through the yeast cap, the cup is filled and poured into glasses without a drop spilled!

What is Vermouth?

Vermouths are perhaps the most ancient of treated wines. They are produced by steeping or soaking wines in flavorful aromatics. Ancients flavored wines with everything from pepper to poppies. Vermouth is from the German for wormwood, a popular flavor. French type vermouth is white and dry. Italian is rich, red and bitter sweet.

What are Vermouth Herbs?

Vermouth comes from the word WERMUT which means man's strength! Ancient man believed firmly that his well-being was served by the myriad of herbs about him. This wine is flavored by as many as forty of nature's cures including allspice, cinchona, elder flowers, hyssop, marjoram, anise, cloves and orange peel. No wonder this aperitif stimulates the appetite.

What is a Vigneron?

In France, the wine grape farmer and the wine maker are both called the *vigneron*. These artisans number one and a half million out of a total forty million population. They produce twenty five percent of the entire agricultural income, and literally support a nation where every third family depends on wine. *Vive le vigneron!*

What is the Vinegar Fly?

The dreaded ACETO-BACTER, a microscopic bacteria, present in all wines, is familiarly called the vinegar fly. In the presence of air, it causes a secondary fermentation eliminating the ethyl alcohol making fine vinegar from fine wine. So, keep opened wines capped and in the refrigerator!

What is Vineland?

Leif Ericson and his hardy band touched our shores nearly one thousand years ago. To their surprise and delight, they discovered a profusion of grapevines. They dubbed our country, Vineland The Good, a name which lasted for 600 years in Icelandic literature!

How Many Vinifera Grapes?

The great wine grapes of the world fall into the classification called *vitis vinifera*. Translated literally, that is the vine that grows wine. A warm climate species, there are over five thousand types identified with many more thousands of local names. About two hundred are grown regularly for the wine trade.

What is Vitis Vinifera?

V

Vitis Vinifera is called the vine that grows wine. The native European vines have been cultivated at least five thousand years and propagated to all warm climates on the globe between 35 degrees south and 50 degrees north latitude. All great wines are vinifera!

What is a Vintage?

The practice of marking the vintage year on wine labels confuses most novices. It needn't. Technically, it means no more than a harvest. The grapes were grown in that specific year. There is no relation to quality — good or bad. Vintage charts and guides provide the guesses of the experts at harvest time and are often unreliable. Trust your wine merchant or trust to luck, but don't worry too much about the year.

V

What is Viticulture?

Viticulture is the science — and the art — of grape growing. Grapes are consumed commercially in more forms and in greater amounts than any other fruit of the earth. As fresh fruit, as preserves, as dried raisins, in cans or as wine and brandy, grapes yield a treasury of vitamins and minerals. Vive le viticulturist!

What is Vitis Labrusca?

The easiest way to distinguish the two great families of grapes is by the climates in which they thrive. The profusion of grape vines discovered by the Vikings in North America were of the Labrusca breed. They withstand the heavy winters and produce lovely jams, jellies and juices but lesser wines.

What is Vodka?

The Russian's "dear little water" has become the favorite potable spirit of the American citizen. Vodka is truly the least of all potables as it is taken from the still above 190 retaining nothing of the taste and smell of the grain. This neutrality and ability to mix with anything has propelled Vodka to the top of the charts!

What is V.S.O.P.?

The VSOP designation is found on cognac labels and other French Brandies. In Cognac, there is a bewildering array of items to classify the brandy. Very Superior Old Pale — VSOP — is a step better than Three Star Cognac.

W

What is Whiskey Aging?

Whiskey aging is essentially a mellowing process; it is accomplished in wooden barrels which impart both color and tannin to the spirits. Charred oak barrels are essential to bourbon while softer used barrels create the light Canadian blends. Once bottled, aging ceases!

What is a Whiskey Bead?

Never at a loss for a measure of value, the early whiskey consumer learned to take a bead on the quality of his purchase. When poured in a glass or shaken in a jar, liquor should leave a string-like necklace of bubbles—the bead. The higher the proof, the longer lasting and more uniform the bead!

What is Blended Whiskey?

Blended whiskey—like coffee, tea and tobacco—is a highly refined mix tailored to taste. Blends are works of art which provide the unique tastes to favorite brands. They may include light and heavy whiskies as well as neutral spirits and sherry. Praise to the blender!

What is Body in Whiskey?

The body or thickness of any fluid is easily sensed on the tongue. In whiskey, the size of the original grain is the principle determining factor. The larger the grain, the lighter the resulting whiskey. Hence, Rye with small grain makes bigger bodied whiskey than the larger corn used in bourbon!

W

What is Bonded Whiskey?

Don't be fooled by that stamp. Bottling in bond has nothing to do with quality. An Act in 1894 allowed distillers to skip immediate payment of taxes on bonded bottles. Your only guarantee is that it is straight whiskey, taken from the still below 160 proof, aged at least four years, and bottled at 100 proof. Despite all this, it's usually a bargain!

What is Corn Whiskey?

The distinctive taste of bourbon emanates from the mash and the new charred oak barrel aging. A country cousin of bourbon corn whiskey is of inestimably greater charm. Its ingredients must be eighty percent corn and the aging is accomplished in softer used barrels.

What is Canadian Whisky?

Corn, rye, wheat and barley are used to make the Canadian distillates. However, as in Scotland, the Canadians drop the E from the end of the word and utilize used barrels which impart much softer flavors in aging. Canadian whisky is light and mellow.

What is Light Whiskey?

Light whiskey is the American distillers answer to the lighter Canadian blends. Taken at the very high proof from 161 to 189 from the still and aged in used barrels like the Canadians, the whiskey obtains fewer wood extractives and a mixable taste. It's in the trend to lightness.

What is Rye Whiskey?

Rye was the main crop of our industrious Scottish ancestors. They always set aside a portion for home distilling. Rye and barley produce the strongest tastes in whiskey. Rye whiskey must be produced at least 51 percent from rye grains. Expect the most in taste from Rye. You won't be disappointed!

What is Sour Mash Whiskey?

In sour mashing, each new batch of mash contains about 25% of spent mash from a completed fermentation. It is innoculated then with a lactic culture and this, plus longer fermentation, produces the characteristic bitter-sweet taste in the whiskey.

What is Straight Whiskey?

The simplest definition of straight whiskey is that spirit taken directly from the still — as the white lightning of the moonshiner. Federal rules define straight whiskey as that distilled at 160 proof or under — assuring a strong character — which is aged two years in new charred oak barrels. The trend is away from this strong spirit to the blends and even lighter white spirits.

What is Tennessee Whiskey?

Though made with corn and distilled at low proof, Tennessee whiskey is distinct from bourbon. Its unique body and taste derive from a ten-day torturous journey down through a huge vat packed tight with maple tree charcoal. Try it over ice or sip straight.

What is Wine Acidity?

The most prominent characteristic of wine or any other fruit juice is acidity. Fruits and juices lacking in acidity are flat, dull and insipid. There are generally two classes of fruit acid—volatile and fixed. The volatile smells like vinegar. The fixed is actually a combination of tartaric, malic and citric acids. Every great wine has a good acid level.

What is Wine Bitterness?

Identify bitterness with the red wines. Bitterness in wine is caused primarily by the tannin extracted from the skins during fermentation. This gentle bitter astringency is an acquired taste difficult for new wine consumers. The tannins create the taste complexities of the truly great red wines.

What is Wine Body?

The body or viscosity of wine (as in all other fluids) is its weight or resistance to being poured. In wine a complex inter-marriage of alcohols, suspended solids, tannins and aldehydes render some heavy or full on the tongue, and others light like white wines. Aged wines tend to fuller body.

What is a Wine Bottle?

The very word bottle is a corruption of the French word for wine vessel. Though blown glass was used two thousand years earlier, at about 1680 the cork was first utilized as a wine bottle stopper and the incredible effects of wine-bottle aging achieved. Few realize that wine is the only food to grow and physically improve once bottled! A unique symphony of vintner, cork and bottle create living poetry!

What is Wine Bouquet?

Twirl the glass gently throwing the wine around the sides of the bowl. The profusion of odors that arise are called Bouquet by the wine lover. Few foods offer the complexity and range of smells — from strawberries to musty oak — from lilacs to almonds. The slow oxidation of fruit alcohols, acids and other compounds creates a sensory symphony in great aged wines!

What is Wine Breathing?

Don't be confused or distressed about how long a wine must breathe! Wine breathing is purely and simply the oxidation or browning of the fruit juice similar to a cut apple. The glory and wonder results when this process creates enticing odors and suppleness in aged wines. As a rule reds need more breathing to reach perfection — up to an hour. Just remember, open the bottle early and pour out a bit to break the seal — and let nature take over!

What is Breed in Wine?

One of the most difficult tasks in life is to describe things we taste. The wine connoisseur must employ poetic license to capture the delicate nuances of a particular vintage. However, whether in horseflesh or in good wine, breed is easily understood as the class of the field. A wine of great breed has delicacy, finesse and great character.

What are Wine By-Products?

It is said that the grape is the richest of all fruits because of its deep and ranging root structure. The consequence of this abundance was seen in the second world war when the by-products of grape and wine making ranged from cooking powders and salts, to shoe tanning, to potato chips, to soap making, to synthetic rubber and a host of similar commercial products.

What is Wine Complexity?

Wine lovers nearly always advert to poetic terms to express profound reaction to superb vintages. Opaque, velvety, well-rounded, and elegant are common terms. Complexity involves the range of human sensations and it derives from the sum of all the parts from soil to aging bottle. It is a mystery! It is a symphony!

What is Concord Wine?

The workhorse of the native American grape industry is the Concord grape. A hybrid, as are most American varieties, Concord was first cultivated in 1843 and named for Concord, Massachusetts. Used widely for juice, jams and jellies, it is most noted as a creamy sweet Kosher ritual wine.

What is our Wine Consumption?

Per capita consumption of wine in our land is somewhat more than two gallons per year. It is growing steadily, particularly among young adults who drink five times the wine as their elders. By contrast, the French, Italians and Spanish exceed thirty gallons per year!

What is a Wine Cork?

Pliant, oak bark which prevents destructive air from entering bottle so wine will mature. Discovered in 17th century, corked glass replaced barrels and ancient Greek Amphora. If kept wet with wine, will last for decades.

What are Dessert Wines?

Americans are newly discovering a treasured European practice of serving rich, full-bodied and mellow dessert wines *with desserts*. Ranging in color from the pale gold of the sherries to the tawny and ruby of the ports, the high sugar and alcohol provide appropriate accent to the meal's end.

What is a Dry Wine?

In the wine business, the word dry means no sugar. It's as simple as that. Dry wines have no detectable sugar content. Medium dry wines have a sweet overtone. Sweet dessert wines like Port or Cream sherry have up to fourteen percent sugar by volume. You either like 'em dry or you don't!

What is Fortified Wine?

Though federal authorities have declared the term illegal, Americans still persist in describing their dessert wines as fortified. The age old process of adding clear, high proof brandy to a fermenting tank literally pickles the grapes! High fruit sugar is retained and high alcohol is assured!

What is Foxy Wine?

Foxy wine has no relationship to the clever animal of the same name, though historically the word may have derived from native Fox grapes. Foxy simply refers to an odd, musty odor and flavor in wines caused by methyl anthranilate in indigenous grapes!

What is Generic Wine?

Over the centuries, wines made and shipped from certain geographic areas [such as Burgundy in France] became identified with those areas. The same kinds of wines grown in other countries were then named as Burgundy, Chablis or Sherry. Usually generics are blends of a number of common grapes.

What is Grey Riesling?

Grey Duchess or Grey Riesling is a California grand dame. Search the great wine authorities and you will seldom find this popular, soft white wine mentioned. Whatever its uncertain heritage, it is NOT a member of the popular Riesling family. Accept it for what it is - a popular, slightly sweet California varietal.

What is a Hybrid Wine?

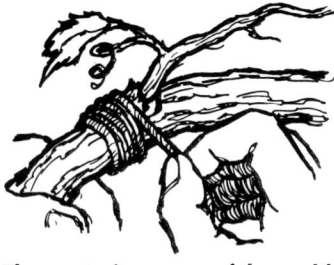

The great wine grapes of the world are native to the warmer portions of the globe. In attempts to cross the hardiness of native American cold climate grapes with the finer varieties, thousands of hybrids have emerged. A few produce distinctive and pleasant wines such as the Ruby Cabernet in California and Baco Noir, Chancellor Noir and Aurora in New York.

What is Kosher Wine?

Kosher wines by Rabbinical law are those produced pure and unmixed under supervision of a Rabbi. By general perception, they are intensely sweet, Concord grape or berry wines. While these types have popularity in America, Kosher wines used in religious festivals may be sweet, dry, table or sparkling. Local custom prevails as to type!

What is May Wine?

During the Dark Ages, wines were flavored with nearly all available herbs both to improve the taste of bitter wines and for medicinal effects. One such blend is still found in German spring festivals. Light wine is flavored with sweet woodruff and strawberries or other fruit is added. Some May wine is bottled and exported. A light delight!

What is Mendoza Wine?

Seven hundred miles inland from the coast of Argentina lies one of the world's most abundant and well organized wine industries. Nestled into the Andean Mountains, the province of Mendoza contains over six hundred fifty thousand acres of grapes — twice that of the United States. Fine varietals imported originally from Europe produce excellent wines.

What is Oxidation in Wine?

You can visualize the effect of oxidation in any fruit by the browning of a cut apple. When the skin of a fruit is broken, the pulp fixes oxygen and releases hydrogen. This is perfectly natural, but equally harmful to the fruit or wine. Sulpher dioxide in minute quantities controls the oxidation of tannins, pigments and minerals. Keep your wines from exposure to air!

What is Wine Pasteurizing?

Among his many contributions to man, Louis Pasteur discovered that yeast and bacteria in fluid are killed or inhibited following brief exposures to high temperatures. Great table wines are never subjected to heat, but beer and many common table and dessert wines are stabilized by pasteurizing!

W

What is the pH in Wine?

Literally, pH is the hydrogen ion content of the wine. Practically, it is the measure of acidity. Balanced wines have a delightful tang and tartness. Acid-deficient wines are flat and uninteresting. The best wines measure between 4 and 5 on the pH scale.

What is Pop Wine?

The ninety percent increase in wine consumption this decade was due to prodigious guzzling by our young of sweet concoctions termed Special Natural Wines. To a nation weaned on sweet soda pop, these fusions of alcohol and fruit juices were naturals. That's why the Pops are so popular!

What is a Piquant Wine?

Wine writers often refer to piquancy, particularly in white wines. The dictionary declares this to be a sharply stimulating sense of taste. It is generally understood to be a sharp but pleasing level of fruit acid.

What Is A Wine Press?

The primary objective of the winemaker is to extract the maximum juice from the grape for fermenting. The press squeezes out rich liquid. From the stomping of the grapes or squeezing them through slatted barrels to the modern pneumatic steel cages, the juice is the goal.

What is quick aged wine?

Once man discovered the unique qualities derived from aging wine, he set about to create short-cuts. Each attempt has been less than satisfactory. These range from immersion of fresh oak chips in the wine vats to literally baking the wines at 120 degrees or more. Great wines all need the gentle harmonizing of time itself!

What is Red Wine?

Anyone who has ever bit the skin or seed of a grape can readily grasp the character as well as the process for fermenting red wines. When left in the fermenting tank, both the color and the bitterness of the skins and seeds are imparted to the wines!

What is Rhine Wine?

In the white wine boom in the American market, nearly everything called Rhine wine is in demand. Imported Rhine wines are those which originate along the Rhine and its tributaries, from the best to the least Liebfraumilch. In America, Rhine wines are dry to medium dry, flowery pleasant but largely undistinguished vintages. In sum, Rhine wines are light and easy whites.

What is Rice Wine?

The popular Saki is often called rice wine since it contains from 12-16% alcohol and is sold in a wine type bottle. This Japanese favorite since the 8th century is actually a beer! It is made by cleaning, steaming and then fermenting rice. Sakamizu means "water of prosperity".

What is Rosé Wine?

While most wine lists carry this popular wine type as a separate category, by classification it is a red wine. It is fermented on the grape skins for a very brief period to obtain the anthocyanin pigmentation but very little of the tannins and heaviness of the reds. In terms of taste and style, the Rose' resembles the light fruitiness of the white wines!

What is a Sparkling Wine?

When a wine is sparkling, it contains from two to six atmospheres of carbon dioxide created by a secondary fermentation. This term covers all types — champagne is white, sparkling burgundy is red, crackling rose' is pink — but they are all sparkling wines.

What is Wine Sediment?

The sediment often found in older bottles of wine results from natural precipitation of crystals and other solids. Wineries today exercise great care in racking and filtering these tartrates, tannins and compounds before bottling . . . all of which are harmless in consumption. If found, carefully decant to another container.

What are Table Wines?

Table or dinner wines quite simply are those vintages designed for consumption at the table with meals. They may be red, white or pink; are usually 12 percent in alcohol and may also range from the perfectly dry or sugarless types to those with a gentle trace of grape sugar. You be the judge. The wines you like are the proper table choices!

What is Varietal Wine?

A wine made from a variety of grapes. Cabernet Sauvignon is a grape variety. By law, there must be at least 51% of that varietal wine in the bottle. You'll love these select, longer aged wines.

What is Vintage Wine?

Don't be confused! A vintage year means only that the grapes were grown in the year on the label. Otherwise, wines are blended from year to year for balance. Vintage wine may be superb or awful. Trust the brand name or ask your friendly wine merchant.

What is X.O. Brandy?

In addition to the well known cognac letter designations as Three Star, V.S.O.P. and Napoleon, there is special designation for a full bodied, fruity spirit titled X.O. Hennessy, X.O. Cognac and the Christian Brothers X.O. Brandy as examples of this complex, rich distillate.

What is a Yard of Ale?

The tavern in ancient times as well as today was the scene of frivolity and practical joking. The yard was one of a series of "puzzle glasses" used to spill the frothy contents on an unsuspecting customer. The yard glass — literally three feet long — emerged as a popular beer glass in its own right. A yard of ale contained over three pints and required great care in the drinking!

y,z

What is Yeast?

Wine lovers the world over praise this tiny, micro-scopic airborne plant life called yeast. A small bucket of working yeast will ignite a twenty thousand gallon vat of grape juice. The yeast consumes the grape sugars creating alcohol and carbon dioxide. Without them, there would be no wines or brews!

What is Chateau d'Yquem?

The first among the great rich Sauternes of Southern France without question is d'Yquem! The grapes are picked very late so that a friendly mold penetrates the skin reducing the fluid and concentrating the sugar. The resulting wine is unbelievably smooth, rich and mellow. Very expensive but truly liquid gold!

What is Zinfandel?

The heritage of the noble red Zinfandel is shrouded in mystery. California grapes with few exceptions are European grapes, transplanted to thrive in the ideal soil and sun. Traditionally used as a blender with other reds, Zinfandel is now emerging as a fine, fruity, light-bodied California varietal--an uniquely American wine!

What is Zubrovka?

Zubrovka is the enormously popular Polish vodka. More like a liqueur than the pure white American vodkas. Zubrovka has an attractive yellow-green tint, a really earthy aroma and slightly bitter taste. All of these derive from soaking the spirit in native Zubra grass, and leaving a blade in the bottle!

The Proof of Things

To maintain perspective in beverage alcohol consumption, recognize the proof or volume of alcohol in the drink.

In the United States we measure proof spirit as exactly twice the alcohol content by volume at a temperature of 60°F. However, beer is measured by the weight of alcohol in the fluid and wine is recorded in the exact amount of alcohol by volume.

Here is a comparison of these three measurements:

BEVERAGE	HOW MEASURED	RANGE OF ALCOHOL	AVERAGE SERVING	APPROX. AMT. OF ALCOHOL
RUM	PROOF	80-151 PROOF	ONE OUNCE @ 151 PROOF	3/4 OUNCE
BOURBON	PROOF	80-100 PROOF	ONE OUNCE @ 100 PROOF	1/2 OUNCE
BRANDY	PROOF	80 PROOF	ONE OUNCE @ 80 PROOF	4/10 OUNCE
LIQUEUR	PROOF	54-100 PROOF	ONE OUNCE @ 60 PROOF	3/10 OUNCE
BEER	WEIGHT	3.5-4%	ELEVEN OUNCE CAN	4/10 OUNCE
DESSERT WINE	VOLUME	18-20%	THREE OUNCES	6/10 OUNCE
TABLE WINE	VOLUME	12-14%	FIVE OUNCES	6/10 OUNCE

Calories...

	Ounces	Approx. Calories
Glass of Milk	8	160
Dry Martini	2	160
Liqueur or Cordial	2	200
Glass of Beer	12	150
Glass of Dry Wine	4	96
Glass of Dry Sherry	3	99
Glass of Cream Sherry	3	120
Glass of Champagne	3	75
Daquiri	2	150
Shot of Bourbon	1-1/4	120

...and sugar levels

Classification	Sugar Range By Volume	Wine Types
Dry Wines	Zero	Pinot Noir, Cabernet, Sauvignon, Chablis, Burgundy, Claret, Pinot Chardonnay
Medium Dry Wines	1% to 3%	Chenin Blanc, Rhines, Light Chablis, Liebfraumilch, Extra Dry Champagne, Dry & Cocktail Sherries, Rose' Wines
Medium Sweet Wines	3% to 5%	Golden Sherry, Sauterne, Champagne Rose, Rose' Wines, Lambrusco
Sweet Wines	7% to 13%	Cream Sherry, Ports, Berry & Fruit Wines, Cold Duck

Beverage Tasting Simplified

A Trio of Tastes

We are born with about ten thousand minute papillae or taste buds on the tongue, the roof of the mouth and in the throat. These sensors discern among tastes much as tiny fingers. As we age, the buds gradually diminish in sensitivity and even in number. The older we become, the less sensitive we are to the nuances of taste

The tip and sides of the tongue respond to sweetness. Saltiness is perceived also near the front and on the sides of the tongue. The back and sides of the tongue and the roof of the mouth deliver both sourness and bitterness. Therein lies the whole complex world of taste—sweetness, sourness, bitterness and saltiness.

As we readily recognize, most foods provide a combination of two or more of these basic sensations. Apples are at once sweet and sour when ripe. Lemons are predominantly acidic or sour but there is an overtone of astringency or bitterness. The persimmon and strong tea are both strongly bitter, but are often consumed with a dash of sugar.

The mouth also warns us of heat and cold; rough and smooth; heavy and light. Syrup is full in body as water is light.

The hormone cortisone regulates taste. Since it flows more abundantly in the mornings, our tastes are more sensitive then. In addition, the buds fatigue easily and are almost as unpredictable as mood swings that afflict us through the day.

In wine and spirit tasting, we are concerned primarily with a *trio of tastes*—sweet, sour, and bitter—since saltiness is rare as a natural commodity in liquors.

Aroma and Bouquet

The olfactory or smell organs are located at the head of the nasal cavity. These extremely sensitive conductors react to molecular gases given off by thousands of objects about us, food included.

Yet, the line often blurs between taste and smell. Close your nostrils and you will have difficulty telling an apple from an onion. Flavor is considered to be a fusion of the two complementary senses.

In wine and spirit tasting, we ascribe particular meaning to two nouns: aroma and bouquet. *Aroma* is the remaining odor of the original fruit or grain. Hence, the aroma of wine is grape smell. *Bouquet* is comprised of a host of odors which are created in the fermentation, distillation and aging processes.

While this may sound a bit technical, it is really quite natural. What we have done is to distinguish fresh fruit odors as aroma, and newly created odors as bouquet.

A Total Human Response

Professionals use the word "organoleptic" to describe the harmonious human response in tasting. Attention to all stimuli can heighten and expand upon the basic tastes and smells. Try to involve these three areas in your personal response to a wine or liquor.

> **Visual:** the basic appearance, the sheen, clarity, the brilliance, the trueness of color.
>
> **The Nose:** the "grapey", or varietal character, in wine or fruit liquors, the smokiness in Scotch, the profusion in wine bouquet, from lilacs and strawberries to apples and pears, the intensity and persistence of each.
>
> **The Gustatory Response in the Mouth:** the body or viscosity, the delicacy or sharpness, the harmony of flavors; the finish or aftertaste.

Some Commonly Used Terms in Tasting

Appearance: overall clarity and sheen

Acidity: the presence of fruit acids as in oranges or grapefruit, the absence of acidity is flatness, and over-acidity is tartness.

Astringency or Bitterness: Astringency is a puckery feeling on the sides and the central portion of the tongue. This sensation is often confused with bitterness which is one of the four tastes. Both occur from the presence of tannin in wines. Distinguish astringency as a tactile feeling and bitterness as a taste.

Body: the thickness of the fluid, the heaviness on the tongue.

Balance: everything seems just right.
Dryness: the absence of sugar.
Flavor: distinct harmony in smell and taste.
Fruitiness: retention of the liveliness of the fruit flavors.
Medium dry to medium sweet: the growing concentration of sugar.
Quality: truly a subjective judgment.

Five Easy Steps to a Relaxed Wine-Tasting Party

STEP ONE: Decide the Size

Every other decision depends upon the number of guests. Invite a few neighbors or an entire social club. You can plan about a half bottle per person over a two hour wine tasting. This presumes six or seven wines and slightly over an ounce per person for each selection. It will average out that way! And your major expense can be figured by planning one bottle of each type for each twenty guests.

STEP TWO: Pick the Place

Choose a patio, a room or a hall, if need be, that accommodates the expected guests and no more! There needs to be room for a supplies table in the entryway, an hors d'oeurves table and, ideally, a table for each wine being tasted. Allow for ease of movement, but create the crowd atmosphere. It will enliven your tasting!

STEP THREE: Pick the Wines

This is an easier task than you might suspect. Since few people consume wine regularly in their homes, the average audience will be pleased whatever your choice. Here are a few suggestions:

Choose no more than seven or eight wines.

Try a mix: three white, two rose', two red, one sparkling.

Contrast three domestic wines with three similar imports.

Contrast three lower priced jugs with three similar premiums.

Try a sparkling tasting: Brut, Extra Dry Champagne Rose', Sparkling Burgundy and Cold Duck.

Try a dessert tasting: Port, Sherry, Tokay, Sweet Vermouth and Muscatel.

Try a Sherry tasting: Dry, Cocktail, Golden, Cream—all sherries.

You can see the combinations are numerous. Whatever the choice, try to follow the rules for order of tasting: dry to sweet, white to red and light to heavy.

STEP FOUR: Assemble the Props

Wine tastings may be elaborate and formal, or simple and relaxed. Remember that the wine is the featured attraction . . . and an enhancement for socializing with friends. Here are the basic materials you'll need:

- One wine glass per person. Glassware is ideal though plastic will do. Tasters keep their glasses through the tasting.

- Water pitchers and plastic buckets for each table so guests may rinse glasses if desired.

- Paper napkins in profusion.

- Pencils and pads, if you plan to rate the wines, or play tasting games.

- Xeroxed list of the wines in the suggested order of tasting with brief comments of what to look for in each wine. Consult the labels or a wine book for descriptions.

- Morsels to clear the palate. These can range from simple breads and cheeses to elaborate canape's—whatever the budget allows—but avoid the spicy and salty.

- Decorate to suit your mood: posters, grapes, leaves.

STEP FIVE: Relax and Let the Wine Work Its Wonders

Don't make a big to-do. Wine tastings ought to be simple, casual, fun events. Allow your guests to socialize and to wander freely between the tables. Educate your wine servers on the basics of the wines being tasted so they can make appropriate comments. Ask them to serve just one ounce or so each time. Stand back and have a good time. The wine will work its magic for you!

Cheese & Wine...
The Happy Marriage

Bear in mind the same logical relationship between food and wine, and you will triumph at the cheese board. A robust beef roast demands a full bodied, tannic red wine for perfect companionship. A delicate crab souffle' works best with a spicy, slightly acidic white wine. The same rules apply with cheese.

The natural alkilinity in cheese is tempered by the abundant fruit acids in wine. In a manner of speaking all wines harmonize with all cheeses. However, you will discover a greater kinship if you marry the harder cheeses with the stronger wines. In like manner, the soft and creamy types fare best with lighter vintages. Finally, avoid sweets and other desserts which dull the taste buds.

Here are some suggested combinations. Experiment until you discover the right marriages, as you did with other foods!

CHEESES	WINES
HARD Cheddar, Gruyere, Ementhal, Provolone	Pinot Noir, Pinot St. George, Chateauneuf du Pape, Chianti
MEDIUM HARD Monterey Jack, Jarlsberg, Colby, Port Salut	Beaujolais, Port, Gamay, Pinot Chardonnay, Dry Sherry
BLUE Roquefort, Gorgonzola, Stilton, Danish Blue	Burgundy, Port, Dry and Golden Sherry
BLAND Muenster, Edam, Samso, Bombel, Tilsit	Cabernet Sauvignon, Beaujolais, Pinot Chardonnay, Sherries, Port

CREAM
Brie, Camambert, Bel Paese, Pont L'Eveque, Fontina

FRESH CREAM
Feta, Boursen, Cottage, Mozzarella

PUNGENT
Limburger, Liederkranz, Bierkase, Reblochon

Chardonnay, Chablis, Johannisberg, Riesling, Grey Reisling, Semillon, Sauvignon Blanc

Sauterne, Liebfraumilch, Chenin Blanc, Gewurztraminer

Port, Sherries, Barbera, Gamay Noir

Cordials and Liqueurs by Taste

MINT
Creme de Menthe   Universal
Pepermint Schnapps   German
Vandermint   Dutch

FRUIT
Sloe Gin   Tart Plum
Framboise (fram-BWAZ)   raspberries
Fraise (FREZ)   strawberries
Cassis (ka-SEECE)   currant
Creme de Banane   bananas
Southern Comfort   peach

TEA
Suntory green Tea   Japanese

VANILLA
Parfait Amour   French

HERB
Ng Ka Pay   Chinese
Chartreuse (shar-TRUSE)   French
Benedictine   French
B & B   French

ORANGE
Cointreau (kwan-TRO)   French
Curacao (cure-a-SOW)   West Indian
Sabra   Israeli
Triple Sec   West Indian
Amer Picon (PEE-kon)   France

CITRUS
Strega   Italian

COFFEE
Kahlua   Mexican

Tia Maria   Jamaican
Creme de Mocha

HONEY
Drambuie (dram-BOO-ee)   French
Irish Mist   Irish

NUTTY
Amaretto   Italian
Creme de Noyaux (know-YO)   French
Persico   English

CHERRY
Cherry Heering   Danish
Kirsch   French
Kirschwasser   German
Wishniak   Polish

CHOCOLATE
Chocolate Marmot   Swiss
Creme de Cacao   Universal
Creme de Chocolate   South African
Afri-Koko   Sierra Leonese
Vandermint   Dutch

ANISE/LICORICE
Anisette   Universal
Pastis   French
Ouzo   Greek
Mastic   Greek
Sambuca   Italian
Galliano   Italian

CARAWAY
Kummel (KIM-el)   Scandinavian
Aquavit   Scandinavian

Know Your Limits

Don't be confused about your ability to hold liquor! Your ability to drive, to swim, to fire a gun or to perform any skilled and dangerous function is impaired to some degree by the consumption of ethyl alcohol in any form.

Alcohol relaxes the central nervous system and thereby slows reactions.

Authorities have clarified this condition in terms of your BAC—BLOOD ALCOHOL CONCENTRATION—literally the amount of the drug that is present within your bloodstream. A BAC level of a tenth of a percent is accepted most places as legal

A Guide to Calculate Your Blood Alcohol Concentration

(One Drink Equals a Shot of Liquor, a Beer or Glass of Wine)

Number of Drinks		1	2	3	4	5	6	7	8
Alcohol % In Blood At Various Body Weights	100 lbs	.029	.058	.088	.117	.146	.175	.204	.233
	140 lbs	.021	.042	.063	.083	.104	.125	.146	.166
	180 lbs	.017	.033	.049	.065	.081	.097	.113	.130
	200 lbs	.015	.029	.044	.058	.073	.087	.102	.117
					Physical Abilities Impaired For Driving or Other Functions			Legally Drunk Concentration	

intoxication. At half that level—a BAC of .05%—inhibitions are lowered and judgment impaired. A one hundred pound person reaches *this dangerous level on the second drink!* As the concentration increases, stability decreases.

Study this chart carefully to determine your maximum consumption level. *Then be conservative and reduce it even more as you are probably in a fatigued and excited condition when socially drinking!* The calculations for the chart were developed at the Center for Alcohol Studies, Rutgers University. The chart has been widely distributed by law enforcement authorities.

DON'T TAKE CHANCES...
TAKE TIME BEFORE DRIVING

Alcohol is "burned up" by your body at .015% per hour, as example, a 180 lb. person who consumes eight drinks in four hours has concentrated up to .130% of alcohol in the bloodstream and has oxidized only .060% leaving an impaired driving level of .070% in the bloodstream.

All That's Needed in Glassware and Equipment

Limitations in storage space and the fragility of most glassware are realities of life. The average kitchen soon abounds in mismatched units. To solve these universal problems, a little imagination and a penchant for uniformity of style will suffice. First, do not succumb to the exotic unless your budget for re-stocking is unlimited. Purchase sturdy, clear glassware. It's easier to match and allows greater visual appreciation for the creamy liqueurs and the happy champagne bubbles. Second, avoid the scallops and cut-glass effects for both of the above reasons. Finally, select a limited number of glass types and preparation tools with universality of use in mind. Here are one man's suggestions for the all purpose, easy to substitute home bar.

Tools of the Trade

While often neglected, a simple ice tongs is an ecological necessity to avoid dirty digits in the ice bucket. Choose that ice bucket to serve also as a wine cooler for whites and bubblies, and make sure it has a lid to slow the ice melting. A nice, but not really necessary touch is provided by a standard lemon/lime squeezer and it's flashy to use. Of course, the basic 1½ ounce (50 milliliter) shot glass is required with the one ounce pour line. An abundance of both good and useless corkscrews are available. We recommend the standard waiter's tool for every household. It is easy to master and the narrow steel worm seldom destroys the fragile cork. A relatively new style, with the double prongs works like a charm and preserves the cork intact for re-use. For other implements utilize standard kitchen utensils to stir, cut and serve.

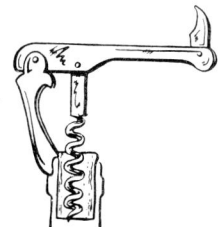

Universal Glassware

The handy, dandy, and attractive ten to thirteen ounce Old Fashioned tumbler is the basic glass. For all specialty cocktails and 'on the rocks' orders, it suffices and it can also double as a fruit juicer for every day use. The nine or ten ounce hiball or Collins glass comes next and is handy for flips and soft drink requests. A nice, quiet elegance is mirrored in the one ounce, straight sided liqueur pony. You need only a half dozen or so and they accompany fine desserts with the perfect *elan*.

For the pre-prandial aperitif and the after dinner dessert wine, I suggest a slant sided sherry glass, but this luxury could be omitted in favor of the absolutely mandatory brandy snifter. Nothing can quite replace the delight of swirling that magical fluid in the bowl over the warming palm, releasing ethereal fumes.

In wine presentation, the trend is to the huge fifteen to eighteen ounce bowls on towering stems with the squat type for red and rose' vintages and the taller type for the whites. For the practical housewife, the standard seven to ten ouncer will work as well, and can be utilized for whiskey sours, ports and sherries. For champagne, buy the tulip style to preserve the bubbles.

Finally, splurge on a half dozen pilsner shells for the brew drinkers. Nothing can beat the attractive and taste provoking two inch head of foam and the glasses serve many other soft drink and wine flip needs.

How to Tend Bar While Smiling and Talking

Bartending is an art not easily acquired. However, the elegant service lies within the reach of all. With the proper equipment recommended earlier, here are a few professional rules of the roost for home parties.

1. Limit the selection of exotic mixed drinks and prepare carefully all the ingredients and equipment in advance of the party. The style of the party or the time of the

year will dictate the selection — Daiquiris, Cuba Libras in August instead of Hot Buttered Brandy and wine mulls. Of course, the standard hiball and juiced selections should be available no matter the occasion.

2. Always measure your drinks — exactly according to the recipe book. Your guests appreciate the balance and style of favorite libations. Over-pouring or sloppy measurements are sure ruination.

3. Go first class and use fresh fruit and squeezed juices, as well as the best sodas and mixers. The best in booze can be lost in tasteless mixers. Fruit garnishes should be cut thick, up to a quarter of an inch so they don't curl in the glass. Twist rinds must be cut clean of the white matter. Be certain to wipe the entire rim of the glass before TWISTING to release a drop or two of oil over the surface of the finished drink. Oil cuts the hotness of the alcohol, mellowing the drink.

4. For sweetened cocktails such as the Old Fashioned, avoid confectioners sugar. It contains cornstarch that will cloud the drink. Simple syrup is best and easily made, as described in an earlier feature. If granulated sugar is chosen, dissolve the sugar first in a splash of soda before the other ingredients are blended.

5. Stir gently and in a circular motion. Agitation aerates and flattens the beverage, particularly if carbonated.

6. By contrast, when shaking, give it all you've got! Egg, milk, liqueurs and the like require violent action to emulsify into the creamy, foamy delights that satisfy both eye and palate.

7. Chill cocktail glassware — an hour or so in the refrigerator or five minutes in the freezer. It improves the looks, and the tastes. For hot drinks, place a spoon in the glass and pour in boiling water for a minute or so. What an improvement!

8. Use fresh ice, and remember ice will pick up odors from accompanying foods in the freezer. A quick cold bath will freshen it. Cracked or frappe' ice can be made in a kitchen food mixer, or hammered into shape inside a towel.

9. Remember the common measurements called for in cocktail mixes and stick to them: jigger - 1½ ounces; pony -1 ounce; dash - 1/16 teaspoon; wineglass - 4 ounces; tablespoon - ½ ounce; cup - 8 ounces.

Of course, practice a few times with the unusual concoctions to gain facility in preparation. Finally, here are a few housekeeping tips. Place a toothpick through olives, onions and the like and use cherries with stems. Much easier to remove and consume that way. Rub the lips of pouring bottles with wax paper and the drops will disappear. Figure about twenty individual drinks per full liquor bottle. Add carbonated beverages just before serving to preserve the bubbles. For the rest, relax and enjoy yourself behind the bar. Your guests will follow suit!

In Case You Wanted to Ask More About . . .

Brews

U.S. Brewers Assoc. Inc.
1750 K Street N.W.
Washington, D.C. 20006

Brewers Assoc. of America
541 Randolph St.
Chicago, Illinois 60601

Wines

The Wine Institute
165 Post Street
San Francisco, Ca. 94108

Wines & Vines
703 Market Street
San Francisco, Ca. 94103

National Association of Alcohol
Beverage Importers
1025 Vermont Ave. N.W.
Washington, D.C. 20005

The Wine Museum
633 Beach Street
San Francisco, Ca. 94109

The Wine Appreciation Guild
1377 Ninth Avenue
San Francisco, Ca. 94122

Les Amis du Vin
2302 Perkins Place
Silver Spring, Md. 20910

The Wine Spectator
4017 Brant Street
San Diego, Ca. 92103

Foods & Wines From France
1350 Avenue of the Americas
New York, N.Y. 10019

Champagne Information Bureau
522 Fifth Avenue
New York, N.Y. 10036

German Wines Information
Bureau, Third Floor
99 Park Avenue
New York, N.Y. 10016

Italian Wine Promotion Center
One World Trade Center
Suite 2057
New York, N.Y. 10048

Swiss Wine Growers Assoc.
Swissmart, Inc.
444 Madison Avenue
New York, N.Y. 10022

And Spirits

Californian Brandy
Advisory Board
235 Montgomery Street
San Francisco, Ca. 94104

Distilled Spirits Council
of the United States
425 13th Street N.W.
Washington, D.C. 20004

Rums of Puerto Rico
666 Fifth Avenue
New York, N.Y. 10019

Association of Tequila Prod.
World Trade Center Suite 147
P.O. Box 58083
Dallas, Texas 75258

Licensed Beverage Industry
485 Lexington Avenue
New York, N.Y. 10017

Or Some Excellent Books

Wine, An Introduction,
Second edition
M.A. Amerine and V.V. Singleton
Univ. of California Press, 1976

Wines, Their Sensory Evaluation
M.A. Amerine and E.B. Roessler
W.H. Freeman, 1979

Alexis Lechine's Encyclopedia of
Wines and Spirits, Alexis Lechine,
Knopf, 1974

Wine and Your Well-Being,
Salvatore Lucia, Popular Library, 1971

How to Test and Improve Your Wine
Judging Ability, Marcus Irving, Wine
Publications, 1974

The Alcohol Republic
W.J. Rorabaugh
Oxford University Press, 1979

The World Guide to Beer
Michael Jackson
Prentice Hall, 1977

The World Guide to Spirits and
Aperitifs and Cocktails
Tony Lord
Sovereign Books, 1979

Read Those Labels Carefully With These Tips in Mind

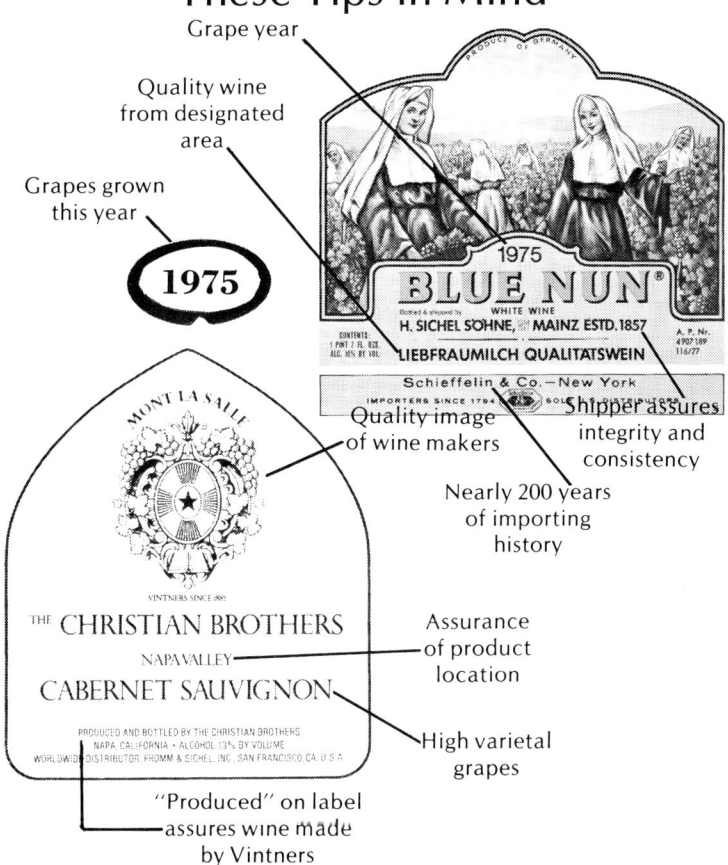

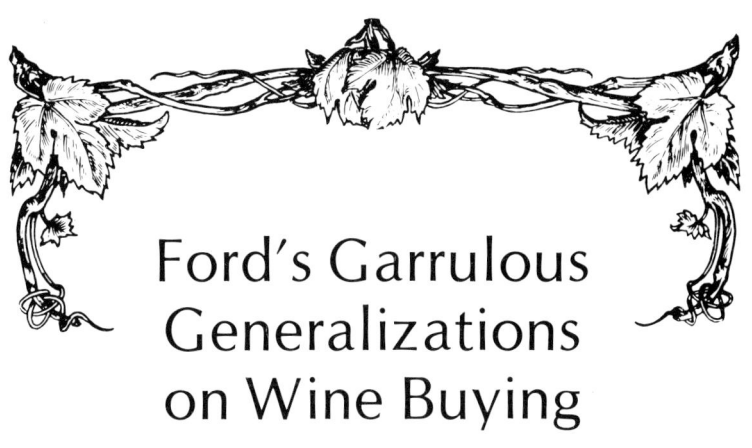

Ford's Garrulous Generalizations on Wine Buying

Everything to this page has been fact. The following is editorial comment. Few other classifications of potable beverages carry the burden of confusion of wines. The range of choices from domestic to import, from premium to price, from generic to varietal, from German to Alsatian, from full-bodied dry red to green-straw white, from soft and mellow to steely, tart Johannisbergs — all of these ranges and choices discourage the novice wine consumer.

No other factor so inhibits wine consumption as the superabundance of types, styles and labels. Consider by contrast the housewife in search of beer or soda pop. If a favorite brand is out, many other substitutes will suffice for there is a general sameness about beer, soda and tomato juice. Remember, these are generalizations! From this broad perspective, brews, sodas and milks are more akin to each other than German and Alsatian vintages of the very same Riesling grapes, not to consider the ranges in tastes of the same wines from Monterey, Napa and San Juaquin counties in California.

Let's face it. The new consumer needs some easy handles and with the temerity of the foolhardy, here are mine that have helped during a decade of professional experimentation. First, semanticists agree that words describing foods mean different things to different people. If one person likes the style of a food or wine, he will use positive words, such as distinctive or assertive. Another judging the same item will advert to it as harsh and unpleasant. In wines, judge *for yourself* and recognize that you bring to the glass your own set of very personal, but very comfortable, prejudices. There are no absolutely right wines, though quite demonstrably there are some very bad ones. Since wines are foods, the beauty is in the eye, or in this case, the palate of the beholder.

Since wines are so diverse, chart some logical path and make a conscious effort to record the results of your experimental tastings

— through all the wines of a company you seem to like; through all the same type of wines in your market; through domestic and imports in the same class; through price and premium. Don't get stuck in one jug. There are many pleasant surprises waiting for you out there.

Attend as many wine tasting parties as you can. But don't forget a little pad to record your reactions on the spot. You'll never remember the nuances later.

As price goes down, sugar goes up. Not universal, but the price wines appeal is to the natural sugar taste in America. Not a bad idea at all for the propagation of the industry in a country that consumes per capita in excess of 100 lbs. of sugar annually.

As price goes up, the style of winemaking more closely resembles traditional European. The Chenin Blanc resembles Saumur and Vouvray as Pinot Chardonnay resembles Montrachet. Premium wines are made from more costly grapes, are not pasteurized and are aged to develop character. Price wines are, generally, from lesser grapes and pasteurized for stability. You get what you pay for in wines.

Most German imports, generics such as Liebfraumilch and Moselblumchen or varietals such as Riesling and Gewurztraminer tend to the sweet side. Used often as aperitif or sipping wines in their homeland, they gratify the sweet teeth of Americans, and the Germans are very smart wine salesmen!

With the notable exceptions of specialty wines such as Cold Duck and Lambrusco, red wines tend to dryness. American vintners currently are experimenting with lighter, mellower reds — the Beaujolais, some Zinfandel and the Rose of Cabernet and Pinot Noir. Search out these lighter reds as logical transitions from exclusive white consumption.

Americans talk dry and drink sweet. The amount of residual sugar has no intrinsic relationship to quality, only style. Ancient wines contained large amounts of natural sugar. Europeans love their sweet table and dessert wines. Don't be embarrased about your level of appreciation in wine. You wouldn't be about sugar in your coffee or the marzipan for dessert.

Pay no heed to the wine snob's derogation of dessert and aromatized varieties. Recovering from the 'wino' image, port, sherry, the vermouths and many other delightful sipping specialties are emerging as appropriate accompaniments to desserts and light foods.

Finally, as the Romans were wont to say — *degustibus non est disputandum* — there is no disputing of taste. Whatever your personal proclivity, there's a wine out there to match it.

Pronunciation of Common Words

ADVOKATT ahd-vo-KHAT
Egg nog liqueur
ALEMBIC ah-LEM-bic
French pot still
AMONTILLADO ah-mon-tee-AH-do
Spanish dry sherry
ANISETTE ahn-i-SET
Licorice liqueur
ANJOU ahn-ZHEW
French white wine
APERITIF ah-pear-ih-TEEF
Before meal wine
AQUAVIT ah-kwa-VIT
Caraway flavored spirit
AUSLESE ows-LAY-zay
Wine from selected grapes
BARBERA bar-BEAR-uh
Dry red varietal
BEAUJOLAIS bo-zho-LAY
Light red varietal
BIKAVÉR beak-ah-VARE
Hungarian red "bull's Blood"
BODEGA boh-DAY-ga
Spanish wine cellar
BORDEAUX bor-DOE
French wine district
BROUILLY brew-YEE
French beaujolais
BRUT brute
Dry champagne
CABERNET SAUVIGNON sew-veeh YAWN   *Dry French red Claret*
CACAO ka-COW-oh
cocoa bean liqueur
CALVADOS COL-va-dose
French apple spirit

COMPARI comPARee
Italian aperitivo
CASSIS kah-SEECE
Currant liqueur
CHABLIS sha-BLEE
Dry white wine
CHAMBERTIN sham-bear-TAN
French dry burgundy
CHARDONNAY shar-doe-NAY
Dry white wine
CHAPTALISATION shaptilly-ZAY-shion   *Addition of cane sugar to must*
CHATEAUNEUF DU PAPE sha-toe-NOOF-du-POP
French dry red Rhone wine
CHENIN BLANC sheh-nin-BLANH
Medium dry white wine
CONGENGER KHAN-gen-er
Taste element in liquor
COTE d'OR coat-DOOR
French burgundy section
CRU crew
French vineyard growth
CYNAR CHE-nahr
Italian artichoke liqueur
DOUX dew
French for sweet
EAU DE VIE oh-duh-VEE
Water of life
FINO FEEN-oh
Spanish dry sherry
FRAPPE' fra-PAY
Liqueur over crushed ice
FRIZZANTE Friz-AHN-tea
Italian semi-sparkling
GAMAY gam-MAY
Light red varietal

GEWURZTRAMINER geh-VERTS-trah-MEEN-er *Spicy German white*
GRAVES grahv *Bordeaux wine district*
GRENACHE greh-NAHSH *Red wine varietal*
HAUT MEDOC oh-meh-DOCK *Bordeaux wine district*
LAMBRUSCO lamb-BROOS-co *Medium sweet Italian red*
LIQUEUR li-CURE *Sweet spirit*
LOIRE la-WHAR *French wine river*
MARC mar *French for grape pressings*
MARGAUX mar-GO *Bordeaux wine*
MEURSAULT mehr-SOH *French chardonnay wine*
MEZCAL mezz-CAHL *Common Mexican spirit*
MIS-EN-BOUTEILLES miz-ohn-boo-TAY-uh *French for estate bottles*
MONTRACHET mohn-rah-SHAY *French burgundy*
MOUSSEUX moo-SUE *French sparkling wine*
MUSCAT muss-KOT *Popular dessert wine grape*
NEBBIOLO neb-ee-OH-low *Italian red varietal*
NOYAUX no-YOH *Almond flavor liqueur*
ORDINAIRE ord-in-NAIRE *French for ordinary*
ORVIETO ohr-vee-AYE-toe *Italian white wine*
OUZO OOZE-oh *Anise liqueur*
PAUILLAC po-YACK *Red bordeaux wine*
PERNOD pear-KNOW *French anise spirit*
PINOT NOIR pee-no-NWHAR *Red wine varietal*

POMMARD po-MAR *French red burgundy*
POUILLY FUISSE' poo-yee-FWEE-say *French white burgundy*
POUILLY FUME' poo-yee-FUME-aye *French white Sauvignon Blanc*
POUSSE-CAFE' poose-ka-FAY *Layered cordials*
PULQUE puhl-KAY *Mexican cactus beer*
QUINTA KEEN-tah *Portuguese vineyard*
RETSINA rhet-SEEN-uh *Greek resin flavored wine*
RHEINGAU rine-GOW *German wine district*
RIESLING REES-ling *White wine varietal*
RIOJA ree-OH-ha *Spanish wine district*
SAINT-EMILION santa-ME-LEE-on *Bordeaux wine district*
SAUMUR sew-MOOR *French white wine*
SAUTERNE so-TAIRN *Soft white wine*
SCHNAPPS shnopps *Dry white spirit*
SEMILLON seh-MEE-yohn *Soft white varietal*
SAOVE so-AH-vay *Italian white wine*
SOMMELIER sohm-may-YAH *Wine steward*
SPATLESE SHPATE-lay-zah *German late picked grapes*
VALPOLICELLA val-po-lih-CHEL-la *Italian red wine*
VARIETAL vah-RYE-eh-tal *Specific variety of grapes*
VINHO VERDE VEEN-vo VAIRD *Portuguese wine district*
VOUVRAY voo-VRAY *French white Loire wine*
CHATEAU d'YQUEM dee-KEM *French sweet white wine*

Index of Questions by Category

BREWS
Ale, 30
Bamberger Rauchbier, 36
Beer Adjuncts, 36
Beer Barrel, 37
Bock Beer, 37
Dark Beer, 37
Dehydrated Beer, 37
Draught Beer, 38
Beer Flavor, 38
Beer Foam, 38
Beer Grains, 39
Krausened Beer, 39
Lager Beer, 39
Beer Life, 39
Light Beer, 40
Near Beer, 40
Beer Pasteurization, 40
Weiss Beer, 40
Bucket of Suds, 44
Cold Lagering, 67
Hops Effect, 64
Hop Flower, 64
Kvass, 66
Malt Liquor, 71
Malted Grain, 71
Mash, 72
Pilsner, 80
Porter, 82
Pulque, 86
Stout, 95
Yard of Ale, 115

CORDIALS
Absinthe, 28
Advocaat, 28
Amaretto, 31
Anisette, 32
Anisone, 32
Aquavit, 33
Benedictine, 41
Bitters, 41
Chartreuse, 47
Cointreau, 49
Cordial, 50
Creme, 50
Curacao, 51
Digestif, 53
Falernum, 56
Fraise, 58
Sloe Gin, 60
Grenadine, 62
Kirschwasser, 65
Kummel, 66
Liqueur, 69
Liguore D'Or, 69
Maceration, 70
Mandarine, 71
Maraschino, 72
Mastikha, 72
Ocha, 77
Ouzo, 78
Pastis, 78
Persico, 79
Poire Williams, 81
Pousse Cafe, 83
Proprietary Cordial, 85
Rock & Rye, 88
Schnapps, 90
Peppermint Schnapps, 90
Slivovitz, 93
Southern Comfort, 93
Simple Syrup, 95
Triple Sec, 98

FERMENTATION & DISTILLATION
Beverage Alcohol, 29
Alcohol by Weight, 29
Denatured Alcohol, 29
Wood Alcohol, 30
Alembic, 30
Al Kohl, 30
Amphora, 31
Aqua Vitae, 34
Bead, 103
Distiller's Beer, 38
Bootlegger, 43
Chaptilization, 46
Color in Liquor, 49
Congener, 50
Cream of Tarter, 50
Criadera, 51
Degree Day, 52
Diatomaceous Earth, 53
Distilling, 53
Triple Distilling, 54
Drip Irrigation, 54
En Tirage, 55
Enology, 54
Enzyme, 55
Fermentation, 56
Malolactic Fermentation, 57
Charcoal Filtering, 57
Flor, 58
Frizzante, 58
Fusel Oil, 59
Grape Bloom, 61
Grape Must, 61
Grape Pruning, 85
Grape Sugar, 61
Heads or Tails, 63
Hogshead, 63
Hydrometer, 65
Proprietary Label, 66
Limestone Water, 68
Liter, 69
Micro Climate, 74
Moonshine, 74
Neutral Spirit, 76
Peat Reek, 79
Pina, 80
Proof Gallon, 84
Oak Char, 76
Oxidation, 111
Pasteurizing, 111
Phylloxera, 80
Proof, 84
Gunpower Proof, 84
High Proof, 84
Ratafia, 86
Sekt, 91
Sherry Vintaged, 92
Solera, 93
Split, 94
Continuous Still, 94
Pot Still, 95
Sugar Acid Ratio, 95
Tail Box, 96
Tete de Cuvee, 97
Ullage, 99
Varietal, 115
Vermouth, 100
Vermouth Herbs, 100
Vigneron, 100
Vinegar Fly, 100
Vinifera Grapes, 101
Vineland, 101
Vintage, 101
Viticulture, 102
Vitis Labrusca, 102
Vitis Vinifera, 101
Whiskey Aging, 103
Breed in Wine, 107
Dessert Wine, 109
Fortified Wine, 109
Kosher Wine, 110

Pop Wine, 112
Wine Press, 112
Quick Aged Wine, 113
Red Wine, 113
Rice Wine, 113
Rose Wine, 114
Sparkling Wine, 114
Table Wine, 114
Vintage Wine, 115
Yeast, 116

TASTING TERMS
Aftertaste, 28
Astringency, 35
Beverage Consumption, 41
Bitterness, 106
Body Temperature, 29
Bocksbeutel, 42
Calories in Wine, 45
Cock & Bull Story, 48
Complexity, 108
Esters, 56
Hangover, 62
Liberty Tree, 68
Olfactory Sense, 77
Palate, 78
Piquant, 112
Pub, 85
Taste Buds, 96
Tip, 97
Wine Acidity, 106
Wine Body, 106
Wine Bottle, 106
Wine Breathing, 107
Who Consumes, 108
Wine Cork, 108
Dry Wine, 109
Foxy Wine, 109
Wine Bouquet, 107
Ph in Wine, 112

SPIRITS
Le Part Des Anges, 68
Arak, 34
Batavia Arak, 34
Armagnac, 34
Asbach Uralt, 35
Bourbon, 43
Brandwein, 43
Brandy, 44
Napoleon Brandy, 44
Pot Still Brandy, 44
Calvados, 45
Cognac, 48
Five Star Cognac, 48
Colonial Flip, 57
First American Spirit, 94

Fish House Punch, 57
Gin, 59
Gin Botanicals, 59
Holland's Gin, 60
Old Tom Gin, 60
Grappa, 61
Grog, 62
Juniper Berry, 65
Liquor Tax, 69
Marc, 71
Martinique Rum, 89
Mezcal, 74
Mull, 75
Muy Anejo, 75
Okolehao, 77
Pisco, 81
Poteen, 83
Rum, 88
Barbados Rum, 89
Puerto Rican Rum, 89
Rum Types, 89
Rumfustian, 90
Scotch, 91
Scotch Blend, 91
Single Malt Scotch, 91
Sling, 93
Teetotaler, 96
Tequila, 97
Uisge Beatha, 98
Vodka, 102
VSOP, 102
Whiskey, Blended, 103
Whiskey Body, 103
Whiskey, Bonded, 104
Whiskey, Canadian, 104
Whiskey, Corn, 104
Whiskey, Light, 104
Rye Whiskey, 105
Whiskey, Sour Mash, 105
Whiskey, Straight, 105
Whiskey, Tennessee, 105
X.O. Brandy, 115
Zubrovka, 116

WINES
Agoston Harazthy, 63
Alsatian Wine, 31
Amontillado, 31
Angelica, 32
A.O.C., 33
Aperitif, 32
Aperitifs, Old, 33
Appellation Controlee, 33
Appetizer Wine, 33

Auslese, 35
Bacchus, 35
Beaujolais, 36
Beaujolais, Premieur, 36
Black Rooster Legend, 41
Blanc de Blanc, 42
Blanc de Noir, 42
Bodega, 42
Bordeaux Wines, 43
Chablis, 45
Champagne Sugar Levels, 45
Champagne Tax, 46
Charmat Champagne, 46
Champagne, Vintage, 46
Chateauneuf Du Pape, 47
Chevaliers Du Tastevin, 47
Chianti, 47
Chieu, 48
Cold Duck, 49
Commandaria, 49
Concord Wine, 108
Cote de Nuits, 51
CRU, 51
Cuvee, 52
Degorgement, 52
Denominazione Di Origine, 52
Deutsche Weinstrasse, 53
Doux, 54
Entre-Deux Mers, 55
Est Est Est, 55
Estufa, 56
Frascati, 58
Generic Wine, 110
Gewurztraminer, 59
Governo, 60
Graves Wine, 62
Grey Riesling, 110
Hermitage, 63
Hospices De Beaune, 64
Hybrid Wine, 110
Jerez Wines, 65
Kiddush Cup, 65
Labrusca, 66
Lacrima Christi, 67
Lambrusco, 67
L'Chayim, 67
Liebfraumilch, 68

Loire Valley, 70
Madeira, 70
Maderized, 70
Marsala, 72
Mavrodaphne, 73
May Wine, 111
Mead, 73
Medoc, 73
Mendoza Wines, 111
Mercurey, 73
Midi, 74
Moselle Wines, 75
Moulin Au Vent, 75
Negociant, 76
Noble Rot, 76
Limousin Oak, 77
Passerilage, 78
Persian Poison, 79
Petite Chateaux, 79
Pineau de Charente, 80
Piquette, 81
Pommard, 81
Porto, 83
Provence, 85
Qualitatswein, 86
Tawny Port, 82
Vintage Port, 82
Wooded Port, 82
Pouilly Fuisse, 83
Quinta, 86
Recioto, 87
Remuage, 87
Retsina, 87
Rheingau, 87
Rheinpfalz, 88
Rhine, 113
Rioja, 88
Sangria, 90
Sediment, 114
Sherry Wine, 92
Fino Sherry, 92
Flor Sherry, 92
Asti Spumanti, 94
Tafelwein, 96
Tokay, 98
Tokaji Azsu, 97
Trockenbeeren Enauslese, 98
Valpolicella, 99
VDQS, 99
Venencia, 99
Wine Byproducts, 107
d'Yquem, 116
Zinfandel, 116